Advanced Latin

13 - question a
14 - a
1.

ADVANCED LATIN

Materials for A2 and Pre-U

Stephen Anderson, James Morwood
and Katharine Radice

Bristol Classical Press

First published in 2009 by
Bristol Classical Press
an imprint of
Gerald Duckworth & Co. Ltd.
90-93 Cowcross Street, London EC1M 6BF
Tel: 020 7490 7300
Fax: 020 7490 0080
info@duckworth-publishers.co.uk
www.ducknet.co.uk

A catalogue record for this book is available
from the British Library

ISBN 978 1 85399 729 7

A teacher's key is available
from the publisher, ISBN 978 185399 730 3

Typeset by Ray Davies
Printed and bound in Great Britain by
CPI Antony Rowe, Chippenham and Eastbourne

Contents

Introduction

Advanced Latin aims to help those studying Latin to A2 or Pre-U. More precisely, we hope that our materials will encourage a disciplined and rigorous approach to language learning, and a broad and imaginative approach to literature.

The language materials fall into three sections. Section 1 consists of 24 translation/comprehension exercises. These are modelled on the language exercises in the new A2 prose and verse papers: each exercise practises the skills of translation, comprehension, grammatical analysis and – where appropriate – stylistic appreciation. In order to match the A2 syllabus requirements, the passages are taken mainly from Caesar, Livy and Ovid and – crucially – we have chosen passages which required minimal adaptation, if any, other than adaptation by omission. We hope, therefore, that these passages will help to smooth the transition from simplified Latin at GCSE and AS to a fuller appreciation of the language at A2.

Each of the translation/comprehension exercises could be tackled as a pure unseen, and thus we hope they will be of use to those preparing for the Pre-U. As a supplement, however, in Section 2 we offer a further six passages for unseen translation. These are, on the whole, more difficult than the passages in the first section, and we hope that they will be useful practice for those aiming for the top end of the Distinction band.

Section 3 contains 12 passages of continuous prose for translation into Latin. Each passage tests a wide range of constructions and idiom, and – in order to help the student – each is supported by notes and suggestions for handling vocabulary, sentence structure, connection and so forth. As an Appendix we provide an English-Latin vocabulary list, which covers all the words used in Section 3. Although primarily targeted at the exercises here, the list would be a good starting point for any students who wish to bolster their English-Latin vocabulary.

The literature materials take a rather different direction. The materials in the language sections should help students to feel more certain in their translation skills and more confident that they understand Latin grammar; the aim behind the literature materials is almost the reverse. Crucial to a deep understanding of any text is – of course – a flexible mind, and a willingness to approach the same passage from different angles. We did not want to offer here a set of notes which might close down thinking, or to pretend that our ideas were the only ideas of value. Instead we wanted to encourage students to think, and then think again, to question whether they really had understood a text or whether there was yet more to understand in its resonances, associations and implications. We wanted to show students that once one angle has been pursued it is worth starting again on a different tack to see if

1

any more can be gleaned. To that end, therefore, in Section 4 we offer explorations on a passage taken from each of the texts set for A2 and Pre-U. These explorations ask more questions than they answer, and they approach the passages using different methods – via context, content, style, parallel texts and so on. The explorations will not 'give the answers', but we hope that they will encourage students to learn to ask themselves the questions which will help them increase their understanding.

The explorations focus necessarily on snapshots of the texts. To help with the whole, Section 5 contains annotated bibliographies. These give a conspectus of the modern works available which are most suitable for literary study at this level (we have avoided writing which is too technical or restricted in its approach). Needless to say, such bibliographies cannot be exhaustive, but we hope that they might be a useful springboard to further reading, and so understanding.

Finally, Section 6 focuses on the Pre-U option for unseen literary criticism. Five passages are given here with questions styled upon those in the Pre-U specimen papers; we have tried where possible to ask questions which leave interpretation open, rather than ask only for a mechanical analysis of a pre-stated effect. We hope that these passages might prove of interest to A2 students too, and perhaps be a happy expansion beyond the prescribed texts.

Stephen Anderson wrote Section 3 and the Prose Composition Vocabulary, James Morwood Sections 4 and 5, and we bear collective responsibility for Sections 1, 2 and 6: in Sections 1 and 6 in particular we collaborated on the choice of passages, but Katharine Radice supplied the questions.

Many people have helped us in writing this volume and to them our thanks are due. Keith Maclennan read through the bulk of the book and made detailed and very helpful suggestions. John Falconer trialled the prose composition exercises. Chris Burnand and John Murrell gave valuable help with the bibliographies. We are grateful too to Stephen Heyworth for letting us use his translations of Propertius in this book and the Key; and to Deborah Blake and all at Duckworth for their help and support in getting us through to publication. We of course take full responsibility for any errors or misjudgements that remain.

Stephen Anderson
James Morwood
Katharine Radice
April 2009

1. Unseen Translation/ Comprehension Exercises

1. Mistaken tactics

Unlike Caesar, Pompey does not make good use of his men's courage.

erat C. Crastinus <u>evocatus</u> in exercitu Caesaris, qui superiore anno apud eum <u>primum pilum</u> in legione decima <u>duxerat</u>, vir singulari virtute. hic signo dato, 'sequimini me,' inquit, '<u>manipulares</u> mei qui fuistis, et vestro imperatori quam constituistis operam date. unum hoc proelium superest; quo confecto et ille suam dignitatem et nos nostram libertatem   5
recuperabimus.' simul respiciens Caesarem, 'faciam,' inquit, 'hodie, imperator, ut aut vivo mihi aut mortuo gratias agas.' haec cum dixisset, primus ex dextro cornu procucurrit, atque eum electi milites circiter CXX <u>voluntarii</u> eiusdem cohortis sunt prosecuti.

inter duas acies tantum erat relictum spatii, ut satis esset ad concursum   10
utriusque exercitus. sed Pompeius suis praedixerat, ut Caesaris impetum exciperent neve se loco moverent aciemque eius distrahi paterentur; idque admonitu C. Triarii fecisse dicebatur, ut primus incursus visque militum infringeretur aciesque distenderetur, atque in suis ordinibus dispositi dispersos adorirentur; leviusque casura pila sperabat   15
in loco retentis militibus, quam si ipsi immissis telis occurrissent. quod nobis quidem nulla ratione factum a Pompeio videtur, propterea quod est quaedam animi <u>incitatio</u> atque alacritas naturaliter innata omnibus, quae studio pugnae incenditur; hanc non reprimere, sed augere imperatores debent; neque frustra antiquitus institutum est, ut signa undique   20
concinerent clamoremque universi tollerent; quibus rebus et hostes terreri et suos incitari existimaverunt.

Caesar, *De Bello Civili* 3.91-2

C. Crastinus, C. Crastini – Gaius Crastinus
C. Triarius, C. Triarii – Gaius Triarius

evocatus, -i, m – veteran
primum pilum duco, ducere, duxi, ductum – I am chief centurion
manipularis, -is, m – soldier
voluntarii, -orum, m – volunteers
incitatio, -onis, f – enthusiasm

(a) Translate *erat C. Crastinus ... prosecuti* (lines 1-9).   [20]

(b) *inter duas acies ... exercitus* (lines 10-11): how much space was left
    between the two battlelines?   [2]

(c) *sed Pompeius ... paterentur* (lines 11-13): what instructions had
    Pompey given his men?   [3]

(d) Explain why *eius* (line 12) must refer to Caesar, not Pompey.   [1]

(e) Give an idiomatic translation of *admonitu C. Triarii* (line 13).   [1]

(f) *distenderetur ... dispositi dispersos* (lines 14-15): what point is
    emphasised here by the repetition of the *dis-* prefix?   [1]

(g) *quod nobis ... videtur* (lines 16-17): quote and translate the words
    which show Caesar thought Pompey's plan was foolish.   [2]

(h) *propterea ... debent* (lines 17-20): what advice does Caesar offer
    military commanders?   [3]

(i) *neque frustra...existimaverunt* (lines 20-22): what was the ancient
    custom and what was its effect?   [4]

(j) Identify the tense of each of the following parts of verbs:
    (i) *esset* (line 10)
    (ii) *distrahi* (line 12)
    (iii) *casura* (line 15).   [3]

2. Terrified flight

As Pompey's men flee in terror, Caesar makes full use of the situation and attacks his camp.

sed Pompeius, ut equitatum suum pulsum vidit atque eam partem, cui maxime confidebat, perterritam animadvertit, aliis quoque diffisus acie excessit <u>protinus</u>que se in castra equo contulit et eis centurionibus, quos in statione ad <u>praetoriam portam</u> posuerat, clare, ut milites exaudirent, 'tuemini,' inquit, 'castra et defendite diligenter, si quid durius acciderit. 5 ego reliquas portas circumeo et castrorum praesidia confirmo.' haec cum dixisset, se in <u>praetorium</u> contulit summae rei diffidens et tamen eventum exspectans.

Caesar Pompeianis ex fuga intra vallum compulsis nullum spatium perterritis dari oportere existimans milites cohortatus est, ut beneficio 10 fortunae uterentur castraque oppugnarent. qui, etsi magno aestu fatigati (nam ad meridiem res erat perducta), tamen ad omnem laborem animo parati imperio paruerunt. castra a cohortibus, quae ibi praesidio erant relictae, industrie defendebantur, multo etiam acrius a Thracibus barbarisque auxiliis. nam qui acie refugerant milites, et animo perterriti et 15 <u>lassitudine</u> confecti, missis plerique armis signisque militaribus, magis de reliqua fuga quam de castrorum defensione cogitabant. neque vero diutius, qui in vallo constiterant, multitudinem telorum sustinere potuerunt, sed confecti vulneribus locum reliquerunt, protinusque omnes ducibus usi centurionibus tribunisque militum in altissimos montes, qui 20 ad castra pertinebant, confugerunt.

Caesar, *De Bello Civili* 3.94-5

Pompeiani, -orum – Pompey's men
Thraces, Thracum – Thracians

protinus – immediately
praetoria porta, praetoriae portae, f – the praetorian gate (i.e. the camp gate nearest to the general's tent)
praetorium, -i, n – the general's tent (i.e. the camp headquarters)
lassitudo, -inis, f – exhaustion

2. Terrified flight

(a) *sed Pompeius … animadvertit* (lines 1-2): what are we told about
     Pompey's forces? [3]
(b) *aliis … diffisus* (line 2): what did Pompey think about the rest of his
     men? [1]
(c) *eis centurionibus … posuerat* (lines 3-4): which centurions does he
     speak to? [2]
(d) *clare … inquit* (lines 4-5): what do you think the prefix *ex* adds to
     the meaning of *exaudirent*? Support your answer by referring to its
     context. [2]
(e) *tuemini … confirmo* (lines 5-6): what is Pompey's battle plan? [2]
(f) *Caesar … oppugnarent* (lines 9-11): how does Caesar's writing
     make it clear that his side has the uppper hand? You should refer
     closely to the Latin and make two points. [4]
(g) *qui … paruerunt* (lines 11-13): what state are Caesar's men in? [2]
(h) Identify and explain the case of:
         (i) *cui* (line 1)
         (ii) *qui* (line 11). [4]
(i) Translate *castra a cohortibus … confugerunt* (lines 13-21). [20]

3. Pompey is killed

Pompey, defeated by Caesar, seeks refuge with Ptolemy,
the boy king of Egypt.

ibi casu rex erat Ptolomaeus, puer aetate, magnis copiis cum sorore
Cleopatra bellum gerens, quam paucis ante mensibus per suos propin-
quos atque amicos regno expulerat; castraque Cleopatrae non longo
spatio ab eius castris distabant. ad eum Pompeius misit, ut pro hospitio
atque amicitia patris Alexandriae reciperetur atque illius opibus in   5
calamitate tegeretur. sed qui ab eo missi erant, confecto legationis
officio liberius cum militibus regis colloqui coeperunt eosque hortari,
ut suum officium Pompeio <u>praestarent</u>, neve eius fortunam despicerent.
in hoc erant numero complures Pompei milites, quos ex eius exercitu
acceptos in Syria Gabinius Alexandriam traduxerat belloque confecto   10
apud Ptolomaeum, patrem pueri, reliquerat.

his tum cognitis rebus amici regis, qui propter aetatem eius in <u>procura-</u>
<u>tione</u> erant regni, sive timore adducti, ut postea praedicabant, sive
despecta eius fortuna, ut plerumque in calamitate ex amicis inimici
exsistunt, his, qui erant ab eo missi, palam <u>liberaliter</u> responderunt   15
eumque ad regem venire iusserunt; ipsi clam consilio inito Achillam,
praefectum regium, singulari hominem audacia, et L. Septimium,
tribunum militum, ad interficiendum Pompeium miserunt. ab his liberaliter ipse appellatus et quadam <u>notitia</u> Septimii productus, naviculam
parvulam conscendit cum paucis suis: ibi ab Achilla et Septimio inter-   20
ficitur.

Caesar, *De Bello Civili* 3.103-4

Ptolomaeus, -i – Ptolemy
Syria, -ae – Syria
Gabinius, -i – Gabinius
Aegyptus, -i – Egypt
Achillas, -ae – Achillas
L. Septimius, L. Septimii – Lucius Septimus

praesto, -stare, -stiti, -stitum – I show
procuratio, -onis, f – management
liberaliter – courteously
notitia, -ae, f – acquaintanceship

(a) *ibi ... expulerat* (lines 1-3): what are we told here about Ptolemy's
     dealings with his sister? [2]
(b) *castraque ... distabant* (lines 3-4): where was Cleopatra? [2]
(c) *ad eum ... tegeretur* (lines 4-6): why did Pompey contact Ptolemy? [4]
(d) *sed qui ... despicerent* (lines 6-8):
     (i) Quote and translate the word which shows that Pompey's
     soldiers acted in a way which Pompey would not have liked. [2]
     (ii) What course of actions did Pompey's men suggest? [2]
     (iii) To whom do *qui* and *eos* refer? [2]
(f) *in hoc ... reliquerat* (lines 9-11): explain how some of Pompey's
     soldiers had come to be in Alexandria? [3]
(g) Give the genitive form of each of the following:
     (i) *casu* (line 1)
     (ii) *castra* (line 3)
     (iii) *milites* (line 9). [3]
(h) Translate *his tum cognitis ... interficitur* (lines 12-21). [20]

4. Plans to leave

The Helvetii make preparations to leave their lands.

ubi se ad eam rem paratos esse arbitrati sunt, oppida sua omnia, numero
ad duodecim, <u>vicos</u> ad quadringentos, reliqua privata aedificia incen-
dunt; frumentum omne, praeterquam quod secum portaturi erant, <u>com-</u>
<u>burunt</u>, ut domum <u>reditionis</u> spe sublata paratiores ad omnia pericula
subeunda essent. persuadent Rauracis et Tulingis et Latobrigis finitimis   5
suis, ut oppidis suis vicisque exustis una cum eis proficiscantur,
Boiosque, qui trans Rhenum incoluerant et in agrum Noricum transier-
ant Noreiamque oppugnaverant, ad se socios sibi <u>adsciscunt</u>.

erant omnino itinera duo, quibus domo exire possent: unum per Se-
quanos, angustum et difficile, inter montem Iuram et flumen Rho-   10
danum, vix qua singuli <u>carri</u> ducerentur; mons autem altissimus
impendebat, ut facile perpauci prohibere possent: alterum per provinciam nostram, multo facilius, propterea quod inter fines Helvetiorum et
Allobrogum Rhodanus fluit isque nonnullis locis <u>vado</u> transitur. extremum oppidum Allobrogum est proximumque Helvetiorum finibus   15
Genava. ex eo oppido pons ad Helvetios pertinet. Allobrogibus sese vel
persuasuros, quod nondum bono animo in populum Romanum vider-
entur, existimabant vel vi coacturos, ut per suos fines eos ire paterentur.
omnibus rebus ad profectionem comparatis diem dicunt, qua die ad
ripam Rhodani omnes conveniant.   20

Caesari cum id nuntiatum esset, eos per provinciam nostram iter facere
conari, maturat ab urbe proficisi et ad Genavam pervenit.

Caesar, *De Bello Gallico* 1.5-7

Rauraci, -orum – the Rauraci
Tulingi, -orum – the Tulingi
Latrobrigi, -orum – the Latobrigi
Boii, -orum – the Boii
Rhenus, -i – the Rhine
Noricus, -a, -um – Noric
Noreia, -ae – Noreia
Sequani, -orum – the Sequani
Iura, -ae – the Juran mountain range
Rhodanus, -i – the Rhone
Helvetii, -orum – the Helvetii
Allobroges, -um – the Allobroges

4. Plans to leave

Genava, -ae – Geneva

vicus, -i, m – village
comburo, -urere, -ussi, -ustum – I burn up
reditio, -onis, f – return
adscisco, adsciscere, adscivi, adscitum – I take to myself, join
carrus, -i, m – baggage cart
vadum, -i, n – shallow water

*

(a) Translate *ubi se ... adsciscunt* (lines 1-8).   [16]
(b) *erant ... possent* (lines 9-12): why was one of the two available
   routes not suitable?   [5]
(c) *alterum ... transitur* (lines 12-14): why was this route much easier? [3]
(d) *extremum ... Genava* (lines 14-16): what are we told about Geneva? [2]
(e) *Allobrogibus ... paterentur* (lines 16-18): how did the Allobroges fit
   into their plan?   [4]
(f) Identify and explain the case of:
   (i) *quibus* (line 9)
   (ii) *animo* (line 17)
   (iii) *die* (line 19).   [6]
(g) Translate *Caesari ... pervenit* (lines 21-22).   [4]

11

5. Druids

As part of his discussion of the two groups of people within
Gaul who are considered far superior to the common
folk, Caesar describes the practices of the Druids.

sed de his duobus generibus alterum est druidum, alterum equitum. illi
rebus divinis intersunt, sacrificia publica ac privata procurant, religio-
nes interpretantur: ad hos magnus adulescentium numerus disciplinae
causa concurrit, magnoque hi sunt apud eos honore. nam fere de
omnibus controversiis publicis privatisque constituunt, et, si quod est   5
admissum facinus, si caedes facta, si de hereditate, de finibus contro-
versia est, idem decernunt, praemia poenasque constituunt; si qui aut
privatus aut populus eorum decreto non stetit, sacrificiis <u>interdicunt</u>.
haec poena apud eos est gravissima. quibus ita est interdictum, hi
numero impiorum ac sceleratorum habentur, his omnes decedunt, adi-   10
tum sermonemque defugiunt, ne quid ex contagione <u>incommodi</u>
accipiant, neque his petentibus ius redditur neque honos ullus <u>commu-</u>
<u>nicatur</u>. his autem omnibus druidibus praeest unus, qui summam inter
eos habet auctoritatem. hoc mortuo aut si qui ex reliquis excellit
dignitate succedit, aut, si sunt plures pares, suffragio druidum, non-   15
numquam etiam armis de principatu condendunt. hi certo anni tempore
in finibus Carnutum, quae regio totius Galliae media habetur, considunt
in loco consecrato. huc omnes undique, qui controversias habent, con-
veniunt eorumque decretis iudiciisque parent. disciplina in Britannia
reperta atque inde in Galliam translata esse existimatur, et nunc, qui   20
diligentius eam rem cognoscere volunt, plerumque <u>illo</u> discendi causa
proficiscuntur.

Caesar, *De Bello Gallico* 6.13

Carnutes, Carnutum – the Carnutes
Gallia, -ae – Gaul

interdico, -dicere, -dixi, -dictum – I forbid, ban from
incommodum, -i, n – misfortune
communico, -are – I share with
illo = illuc

(a) *illi … interpretantur* (lines 1-3): what religious roles do the Druids have? [2]

(b) *ad hos … privatisque constituunt* (lines 3-5): how does Caesar emphasise the Druids' importance? You should refer closely to the language used and make two points. [4]

(c) *si quod … poenasque constituunt* (lines 5-7):
(i) what do the Druids decide when a crime has been committed? [1]
(ii) on what kinds of dispute do the Druids pass judgement? [2]

(d) *si qui … gravissima* (lines 7-9): what is the most severe penalty and for what is it given? [2]

(e) *quibus … communicatur* (lines 9-13): give three details which show how seriously this penalty is taken. [3]

(f) Identify the case of each of the following and then give the corresponding dative form (i.e. if the noun is singular, give the dative singular, if plural, give the dative plural):
(i) *equitum* (line 1)
(ii) *disciplinae* (line 3)
(iii) *praemia* (line 7). [6]

(g) Translate *his autem … proficiscuntur* (lines 13-22). [20]

6. A mysterious oracle

After witnessing a terrifying omen, the tyrant, Tarquinius Superbus,
sends two of his three sons to consult the Delphic Oracle.
The Tarquinii are eager to discover who will hold supreme
power at Rome after their father's death; but their
companion Brutus is cleverer than either of them.

haec agenti Tarquinio portentum terribile visum: anguis ex columna
<u>lignea</u> elapsus cum terrorem fugamque in regia fecisset, ipsius regis
non tam subito pavore percutit pectus quam anxiis implevit curis.
itaque quamquam ad publica prodigia Etrusci <u>tantum</u> <u>vates</u> adhibeban-
tur, hoc velut domestico exterritus visu Delphos ad maxime praeclarum   5
in terris oraculum mittere statuit. neque responsa oraculi ulli alii committere ausus, duos filios per ignotas eo tempore terras, ignotiora maria
in Graeciam misit. Titus et Arruns profecti; comes iis additus L. Iunius
Brutus, Tarquinia, sorore regis, natus, iuvenis summi <u>re vera</u> ingenii,
sed qui simulationem induerat stultitiae, ne ab avunculo interficeretur.   10
is tum ab Tarquiniis ductus est Delphos, <u>ludibrium</u> verius quam comes.

quo postquam ventum est, perfectis patris mandatis cupido incessit
animos iuvenum quaerendi ad quem eorum regnum Romanum esset
venturum. ex infimo <u>specu</u> vocem redditam ferunt: 'imperium sum-
mum Romae habebit qui vestrum primus, o iuvenes, <u>osculum</u> matri   15
tulerit.' Tarquinii ut Sextus, qui Romae relictus fuerat, ignarus responsi
<u>expers</u>que imperii esset, rem summa ope taceri iubent; ipsi inter se uter
prior, cum Romam redisset, matri osculum daret, <u>sorti</u> permittunt.
Brutus aliud ratus significare Pythicam vocem, velut si prolapsus
cecidisset, terram osculo contigit, quod ea communis mater omnium   20
mortalium esset.

Livy 1.56

Tarquinius, -i – Tarquinius
Etruscus, -a, -um – Etruscan
Delphi, -orum – Delphi
Graecia, -ae – Greece
Titus, -i – Titus
Arruns, Arruntis – Arruns
L. Iunius Brutus – Lucius Junius Brutus
Tarquinia, -ae – Tarquinia
Sextus, -i – Sextus
Pythicus, -a, -um – Pythian (i.e. belonging to the oracle at Delphi)

ligneus, -a, -um – wooden
tantum – only
vates, -is, m/f – soothsayer
re vera – in reality
ludibrium, -i, n – object of mockery
specus, -us, m – cave
osculum, -i, n – kiss
expers, -pertis – having no share in, without a part in
sors, sortis, f – lot, fortune, destiny

*

(a) *anguis … fecisset* (lines 1-2): what was the terrifying omen and
     what reaction did it cause in the palace?   [3]
(b) *ipsius regis … curis* (lines 2-3): what was its effect on Tarquinius?   [2]
(c) *itaque quamquam … statuit* (lines 4-6): give two reasons why
     Tarquinius decided to consult the oracle at Delphi.   [4]
(d) *neque … misit* (lines 6-8): why did he choose to send his sons, and
     why do you think he only sent two out of the three?   [4]
(e) *comes … natus* (lines 8-9): what relation was Brutus to Titus and
     Arruns?   [1]
(f) *iuvenis … interficeretur* (lines 9-10): what was Brutus concealing
     and why?   [2]
(g) Identify and explain the case of
     (i) *agenti* (line 1)
     (ii) *Delphos* (line 5).   [4]
(h) Translate *quo postquam … esset* (lines 12-21).   [20]

7. A clever thief

While building the new city of Rome on the Palatine Hill, Romulus offers due worship to the gods and to Hercules, who famously in that very spot had got the better of the thieving shepherd Cacus.

Palatium primum, in quo ipse erat educatus, muniit. sacra dis aliis et Graeco Herculi, ut ab Evandro instituta erant, facit. Herculem in ea loca Geryone interempto boves mira specie abegisse memorant, ac prope Tiberim fluvium, qua prae se <u>armentum</u> agens <u>nando</u> traiecerat, loco herbido ut quiete et pabulo <u>laeto</u> reficeret boves et ipsum fessum via 5
procubuisse. ibi cum eum cibo vinoque gravatum sopor oppressisset, pastor <u>accola</u> eius loci, nomine Cacus, ferox viribus, captus pulchritu-dine boum cum avertere eam praedam vellet, quia si agendo armentum in <u>speluncam</u> compulisset ipsa vestigia quaerentem dominum eo de-ductura erant, aversos boves eximium quemque pulchritudine <u>caudis</u> in 10
speluncam traxit. Hercules ad primam <u>auroram</u> somno excitus cum gregem perlustrasset oculis et partem abesse numero sensisset, pergit ad proximam speluncam, si forte eo vestigia ferrent. quae ubi omnia <u>foras</u> versa vidit nec in partem aliam ferre, confusus atque incertus animi ex loco infesto agere <u>porro</u> armentum <u>occepit</u>. inde cum actae 15
boves quaedam ad <u>desiderium</u>, ut fit, relictarum <u>mugissent</u>, reddita inclusarum ex spelunca boum vox Herculem convertit. quem cum vadentem ad speluncam Cacus vi prohibere conatus esset, ictus <u>clava</u> fidem pastorum nequiquam invocans morte occubuit.

Livy 1.7

Palatium, -i – the Palatine Hill
Albanus, -a, -um – Alban
Graecus, -a, -um – Greek
Hercules, -is – Hercules
Evander, Evandri – Evander (King of the Arcadians, whose city
       Pallanteum was on the site that would later become Rome)
Geryon, Geryonis – Geryon
Tiberis, Tiberis (Acc. *Tiberim*) – the River Tiber
Cacus, -i – Cacus

armentum, -i, n – cattle herd
no, nare, navi – I swim
laetus, -a, -um – rich, luscious
accola, -ae, m – inhabitant
spelunca, -ae, f – cave

7. A clever thief

cauda, -ae, f – tail
aurora, -ae, f – dawn
foras – outwards
porro – onwards
occipio, -cipere, -cepi, -ceptum – I begin
desiderium, -i, n – desire
mugio, -ire – I low, bellow
clava, -ae, f – club

*

(a) *Palatium … muniit* (line 1): what connection did Romulus have to
    the Palatine Hill?   [1]
(b) *Herculem … procubuisse* (lines 2-6): where did Hercules and his
    cattle stop and why?   [5]
(c) *ibi … oppressisset* (line 6): why was it easy for Cacus to steal the
    cattle?   [2]
(d) *captus … vellet* (lines 7-8): why did Cacus want to steal the cattle? [2]
(e) *quia … traxit* (lines 8-11):
    (i) How did Cacus get the cattle into the cave and why did he use
    this method?   [4]
    (ii) Which cattle did he choose?   [1]
(f) *Palatium … traxit* (lines 1-11): within this section, find and write
    out an example of each of the following:
      (i) indirect statement
      (ii) purpose clause
      (iii) gerund
      (iv) a pluperfect subjunctive
      (v) a future participle.   [5]
(g) Translate *Hercules ad primam … morte occubuit* (lines 11-19).   [20]

8. A disastrous love affair

*When Scipio, the Roman commander, demands that Masinissa –
their ally – hand over to the Romans the beautiful Sophonisba,
a Carthaginian woman whom he has impetuously married,
Masinissa contrives a disastrous way to do his
duty to both commander and wife.*

Masinissae haec audienti non rubor solum suffusus sed lacrimae etiam
obortae; et cum se quidem in potestate futurum imperatoris dixisset,
oravissetque eum ut, quantum res sineret, fidei suae temere obstrictae
consuleret – promisisse enim se in nullius potestatem eam traditurum –
ex praetorio in tabernaculum suum concessit. ibi cum crebro suspiritu   5
et gemitu, quod facile ab circumstantibus tabernaculum exaudiri
posset, aliquantum temporis consumpsisset, ingenti edito gemitu fidum
e servis vocat, et venenum mixtum in poculo ferre ad Sophonibam
iubet, ac simul nuntiare Masinissam fidem praestare, ne viva in potestatem Romanorum veniat: memor patris imperatoris patriaeque et   10
duorum regum, quibus nupta fuisset, sibi ipsa consuleret.

hunc nuntium ac simul venenum ferens minister cum ad Sophonibam
venisset, 'accipio' inquit 'nuptiale munus, neque ingratum, si nihil
maius vir uxori praestare potuit: hoc tamen nuntia, melius me mori-
turam fuisse, si non in funere meo nupsissem.' non locuta est ferocius   15
quam acceptum poculum nullo trepidationis signo dato impavide hausit. quod ubi nuntiatum est Scipioni, ne quid ferox iuvenis gravius
consuleret, accitum eum extemplo nunc solatur, nunc quod temeritatem
temeritate alia luerit, tristioremque rem quam necesse fuerit fecerit,
leniter castigat. postero die, ut a praesenti motu averteret animum eius,   20
in tribunal escendit et contionem advocari iussit. ibi Masinissam,
primum regem adpellatum eximiisque ornatum laudibus, aurea corona,
aurea patera, sella curuli et scipione eburno, toga picta et palmata tunica
donat.

Livy 30.15

Masinissa, -ae – Masinissa
Sophoniba, -ae – Sophonisba
Scipio, -onis – Scipio (the Roman commander)

obstringo, -stringere, -strinxi, -strictum – here: I pledge, I give
praetorium, -i, n – military headquarters
tabernaculum, -i, n – tent

18

suspiritus, -us, m – sighing
edo, edere, edidi, editum – I give out
praesto, -stare, -stiti, -stitum – I present, offer
  fidem praesto – I keep my word
impavide – fearlessly
accio, -ire, -ivi, -itum – I summon
luo, luere, lui – I atone for
tribunal, tribunalis, n – speaker's platform
patera, -ae, f – bowl
sella curulis, sellae curulis, f – curule chair (the official seat for
    high-ranking magistrates)
scipio, -ionis, m – staff, sceptre
eburneus, -a, -um – ivory
toga picta, togae pictae, f – an embroidered toga
tunica palmata, tunicae palmatae, f – a tunic decorated with palm branches
    (worn by triumphing generals)

*

(a) *Masinissae … obortae* (lines 1-2): how does Masinissa react?   [2]
(b) *oravissetque … consuleret* (lines 3-4): what does he ask Scipio?   [2]
(c) *fidei* (line 3): explain what this was.   [3]
(d) *ibi … vocat* (lines 5-8): how is Masinissa's grief emphasised? You   [3]
    should refer closely to the Latin used and make three points.
(e) *venenum … veniat* (lines 8-10): why does Masinissa send poison to   [3]
    Sophonisba?
(f) *memor … consuleret* (lines 10-11): what final instruction does he   [4]
    give?
(g) What part of the verb are the following?
    (i) *promisisse* (line 4)
    (ii) *exaudiri* (line 6)
    (iii) *nuntia* (line 14).   [3]
(h) Translate *hunc nuntium … donat* (lines 12-24).   [20]

9. Extreme patriotism

The hero Horatius murders his own sister in anger
at her loyalty to an enemy whom he had killed.

ita exercitus inde domos abducti. princeps Horatius ibat, <u>trigemina</u>
spolia prae se gerens. cui soror virgo, quae <u>desponsa</u> uni ex Curiatiis
fuerat, obvia ante portam Capenam fuit, cognitoque super umeros
fratris <u>paludamento</u> sponsi, quod ipsa confecerat, solvit crines et fle-
biliter nomine sponsum mortuum appellat. movet feroci iuveni animum   5
<u>comploratio</u> sororis in victoria sua tantoque gaudio publico. stricto
itaque gladio simul verbis <u>increpans</u> transfigit puellam. 'abi hinc cum
immaturo amore ad sponsum,' inquit, 'oblita fratrum mortuorum
vivique, oblita patriae. sic eat quaecumque Romana lugebit hostem.'
atrox visum id facinus patribus plebique: sed recens meritum facto   10
obstabat.

moti homines sunt in eo iudicio maxime P. Horatio patre proclamante
se filiam iure caesam iudicare: ni ita esset, patrio iure in filium <u>animad-</u>
<u>versurum</u> fuisse. orabat deinde ne se, quem paulo ante cum egregia
<u>stirpe</u> conspexissent, <u>orbum</u> liberis facerent. inter haec senex iuvenem   15
amplexus, spolia Curiatiorum ostentans, '<u>huncine</u>' aiebat, 'quem modo
decoratum <u>ovantem</u>que victoria incedentem vidistis, Quirites, eum sub
<u>furca</u> vinctum inter verbera et cruciatus videre potestis? i, lictor, <u>colliga</u>
manus, quae paulo ante armatae imperium populo Romano pepererunt.
i, caput <u>obnube</u> liberatoris urbis huius; arbore infelici suspende.' Non   20
tulit populus nec patris lacrimas nec ipsius parem in omni periculo
animum, absolveruntque admiratione magis virtutis quam iure causae.

Livy 1.26

Horatius, -i – Horatius (the sole survivor of the single combats
  between the Horatii and Curiatii)
Curiatii, -orum – the Curiatii (three Latin brothers who have just
  been fought by the three Roman Horatii)
porta Capena, portae Capenae – the porta Capena (a gate in Rome at
  the start of the Appian Way)
Quirites, -ium – Quirites (an official title for the citizens of Rome)

trigeminus, -a, -um – threefold
despondeo, -spondere, -spondi, -sponsum – I promise in marriage
paludamentum, -i, n – a soldier's cloak
comploratio, -onis, f – lamentation

20

9. Extreme patriotism

increpo, -are – I rebuke
animadverto, -ere in + acc. – I punish
stirps, stirpis, f – offspring, progeny
orbus, -a, -um – bereft
huncine = huncne
ovans, ovantis – celebrating, rejoicing
furca, -ae, f – *furca* (a fork-shaped pole to which a criminal's arms were
    tied in punishment)
colligo, -are – I bind
obnubo, -ere, -nupsi, -nuptum – I veil, cover

*

(a) *cui … confecerat* (lines 2-4): why was Horatius' sister distraught? [4]
(b) *solvit … appellat* (lines 4-5): what did her grief cause her to do? [3]
(c) *movet … publico* (lines 5-6): what emotion does the Latin suggest
    Horatius felt and for what reason? In your answer you should quote
    and translate the word(s) from which you can identify his emotion. [3]
(d) *stricto … puellam* (lines 6-7): what did Horatius do? [3]
(e) *abi … hostem* (lines 7-9): how does the language used here reveal
    Horatius' strength of feeling? You should refer closely to the Latin
    used and make two points. [4]
(f) Find in the first paragraph an example of each of the following:
    (i) a participle in the ablative case
    (ii) a pluperfect indicative
    (iii) a present subjunctive. [3]
(g) Translate *moti homines … iure causae* (lines 12-22). [20]

10. Hannibal schemes again

The defeated Hannibal, now living in exile, advises Antiochus III of Syria about a war with the Romans. When he tries to inform his friends in Carthage about what is happening, his messenger is viewed with considerable suspicion.

Hannibal patria profugus pervenerat ad Antiochum et erat apud regem in magno honore, nulla alia arte nisi quod <u>volutanti</u> diu ei consilia de Romano bello nemo aptior super tali re <u>particeps</u> esse sermonis poterat. sententia eius una eademque semper erat, ut in Italia bellum gereretur: Italiam et <u>commeatus</u> et militem praebituram externo hosti; si nihil ibi   5
moveatur liceatque populo Romano viribus et copiis Italiae extra Italiam bellum gerere, neque regem neque gentem ullam parem Romanis esse. sibi centum naves et decem milia peditum, mille equites deposcebat: ea se classe primum Africam petiturum; magno opere confidere Carthaginienses ad rebellandum ab se compelli posse; si illi   10
cunctentur, se aliqua parte Italiae excitaturum Romanis bellum.

in hanc sententiam cum adduxisset regem, praeparandos sibi ad id Carthaginiensium animos ratus, litteras, ne quo casu interceptae palam facerent conata, scribere non est ausus. Aristonem quendam Tyrium <u>nanctus</u> Ephesi expertusque <u>sollertiam</u> levioribus <u>ministeriis</u>, partim   15
donis, partim spe praemiorum oneratum Carthaginem cum mandatis mittit. edit nomina eorum quibus conventis opus esset; instruit etiam secretis notis, per quas haud dubie agnoscerent sua mandata esse. hunc Aristonem Carthagine <u>obversantem</u> non prius amici quam inimici Hannibalis qua de causa venisset cognoverunt. et primo in conviviis <u>cele-</u>   20
<u>brata</u> sermonibus res est; deinde in senatu quidam nihil actum esse dicebant exilio Hannibalis si absens quoque turbare statum civitatis posset.

Livy 34.60-61

Hannibal, Hannibalis – Hannibal
Antiochus, -i – Antiochus
Carthaginiensis, -e – Carthaginian
Aristo, Aristonis – Aristo
Tyrius, -a, -um – Tyrian, of Tyre
Ephesus, -i – Ephesus (a town in Asia Minor)
Carthago, -inis – Carthage

10. Hannibal schemes again

voluto, -are – I turn over in my the mind, consider
particeps, -cipis, m/f – partner
commeatus, -us, m – supply of provisions
nanciscor, nancisci, nanctus sum – acquire, meet with
sollertia, -ae, f – skill, cleverness, ingenuity
ministerium, -i, n – task
obversor, -ari – I appear in public
celebro, -are – I make widely known

*

(a) *Hannibal … sermonis poterat* (lines 1-3): why was Hannibal held in
   such high regard by the king?   [4]
(b) *sententia … geretur* (line 4): what are we told about Hannibal's
   advice?   [2]
(c) *Italiam … Romanis esse* (lines 5-8): explain Italy's importance to a
   foreign enemy and to the Romans.   [4]
(d) *sibi centum … deposcebat* (lines 8-9): what forces did Hannibal ask
   for?   [3]
(e) *ea se classe … bellum* (lines 9-11): why did he ask for them?   [3]
(f) Identify and explain the case of:
   (i) *Italiam* (line 5)
   (ii) *sibi* (line 8).   [4]
(g) Translate *in hanc sententiam … posset* (lines 12-23).   [20]

23

11. An unusual friendship

*To the amazement of the spectators at the Games, a savage
lion greats a slave as an old friend.*

'in circo maximo' inquit 'venationis <u>amplissimae</u> pugna populo
dabatur. eius rei, Romae cum forte essem, spectator' inquit 'fui. multae
ibi saevientes ferae, magnitudines bestiarum <u>excellentes,</u> omniumque
<u>inusitata</u> aut forma erat aut ferocia. sed praeter alia omnia leonum'
inquit 'immanitas admirationi fuit, praeterque omnes ceteros unus. is   5
unus leo corporis impetu et vastitudine terrificoque fremitu et sonoro,
<u>toris</u> <u>comis</u>que cervicum fluctuantibus animos oculosque omnium in
sese converterat. introductus erat inter complures ceteros ad pugnam
bestiarum datus servus viri consularis; ei servo Androclus nomen fuit.
hunc ille leo ubi vidit procul, repente' inquit 'quasi admirans stetit ac   10
deinde <u>sensim</u> atque placide <u>tamquam</u> <u>noscitabundus</u> ad hominem
accedit. tum <u>caudam</u> more atque ritu adulantium canum clementer et
blande movet hominisque se corpori adiungit <u>crura</u>que eius et manus
prope iam exanimati metu lingua leniter <u>demulcet.</u> homo Androclus
inter illa tam atrocis ferae blandimenta amissum animum recuperat,   15
paulatim oculos ad contuendum leonem refert. tum quasi mutua recog-
nitione facta 'laetos' inquit 'et <u>gratulabundos</u> videres hominem et
leonem'. ea re prorsus tam admirabili maximos populi clamores exci-
tatos dicit arcessitumque a Caesare Androclum quaesitamque causam,
cur illi atrocissimus leo uni pepercisset. ibi Androclus rem mirificam   20
narrat atque admirandam.

Gellius 5.14

Androclus, -i – Androclus

amplus, -a, -um – large
excellens, -entis – remarkable
inusitatus, -a, -um – uncommon, unusual
torus, -i, m – muscle
coma, -ae, f – hair
sensim – slowly
tamquam – here 'as if'
noscitabundus, -a, -um – recognising
cauda, -ae, f – tail
crus, cruris, n – leg
demulceo, -mulcere, -mulsi – I caress
gratulabundus – congratulating

(a) Translate *in circo maximo … nomen fuit* (lines 1-9). [20]
(b) *hunc … accedit* (lines 10-12): which details here show that the lion means no harm to Androclus? [2]
(c) *tum … demulcet* (lines 12-14): how do you think the spectators would have reacted to all of this? You should quote and translate three details from the Latin which support your answer. [4]
(d) *homo … refert* (lines 14-16): what did Androclus do once he had recovered his wits? [2]
(e) *ea re … admirandum* (lines 18-21): how is the suprising nature of this story emphasised? You should refer closely to the Latin and make three points. [6]
(f) Identify and explain the cases of:
      (i) *canum* (line 12)
      (ii) *metu* (line 14)
      (iii) *recognitione* (lines 16-17). [6]

12. Biological warfare

The Carthaginian leader, Hannibal, now fighting with King
Prusias of Bithynia against Eumenes of Pergamum,
deploys novel tactics to secure a victory.

classe paucis diebus erant decreturi. superabatur Hannibal navium
multitudine: dolo erat pugnandum, cum par non esset armis. imperavit quam plurimas <u>venenatas</u> serpentes vivas colligi easque in
vasa <u>fictilia</u> conici. harum cum effecisset magnam multitudinem, die
ipso, quo facturus erat navale proelium, <u>classiarios</u> convocat iisque   5
praecipit, omnes ut in unam Eumenis regis concurrant navem, a
ceteris tantum <u>satis habeant</u> se defendere. id illos facile serpentium
multitudine consecuturos. rex autem in qua nave veheretur, ut
scirent, se facturum: quem si aut cepissent aut interfecissent, magno
iis pollicetur praemio fore.   10

tali cohortatione militum facta classis ab utrisque in proelium deduci-
tur. quarum acie constituta, priusquam signum pugnae daretur, Hannibal palam fecit suis quo loco Eumenes esset. rex proelium statim
committere non dubitavit. horum in concursu Bithynii Hannibalis prae-
cepto universi navem Eumenis adoriuntur. quorum vim rex cum sustin-   15
ere non posset, fuga salutem petit, quam consecutus non esset, nisi intra
sua praesidia se recepisset, quae in proximo litore erant collocata.
reliquae Pergamenae naves cum adversarios premerent acrius, repente
in eas vasa <u>fictilia</u>, de quibus supra mentionem fecimus, conici coepta
sunt. quae iacta initio risum pugnantibus concitarunt, neque quare id   20
fieret poterat intellegi. postquam autem naves suas oppletas conspex-
erunt serpentibus, nova re perterriti, puppes verterunt seque ad sua
castra nautica rettulerunt.

Nepos, *Vita Hannibalis* 10.4-11.6

Hannibal, Hannibalis – Hannibal
Eumenes, Eumenis – Eumenes
Bithynii, Bithyniorum – the Bithynians

venenatus, -a, -um – poisonous
fictilis, -e – earthen, made of clay
classiarii, -orum, m – marines, naval forces
satis habeo, -ere, -ui, -itum – I consider it sufficient

(a) *superabatur ... multitudine* (lines 1-2): what problem did Hannibal
    have?   [1]
(b) *dolo erat ... armis* (line 2): what did Hannibal have to do and why? [2]
(c) *imperavit ... multitudinem* (lines 2-4):
    (i) what did Hannibal tell his men to do?   [4]
    (ii) how does Nepos emphasise the quantity of snakes? You should
    refer closely to the Latin and make one point.   [2]
(d) *classiarios ... defendere* (lines 5-7): what was Hannibal's battle
    plan?   [3]
(e) *rex ... fore* (lines 8-10): for what did Hannibal offer a large reward? [2]
(f) *quarum ... Eumenes esset* (lines 12-13): what did Hannibal do
    before battle started?   [3]
(g) Explain why the following are subjunctive:
    (i) *esset* (line 2)
    (ii) *concurrant* (line 6)
    (iii) *daretur* (line 12).   [3]
(h) Translate *rex proelium ... rettulerunt* (lines 13-23).   [20]

13. Grief at leaving home

Ovid recalls with sadness the last night he spent in
Rome before his exile began.

cum subit illius tristissima noctis imago,
    quae mihi supremum tempus in urbe fuit,
cum repeto noctem, qua tot mihi cara reliqui,
    labitur ex oculis nunc quoque <u>gutta</u> meis.
iam prope lux aderat, qua me discedere Caesar   5
    finibus extremae iusserat Ausoniae.
nec spatium nec mens fuerat satis apta parandi:
    <u>torpuerant</u> longa pectora nostra mora.
non mihi servorum, comitis non cura legendi,
    non aptae <u>profugo</u> vestis opisve fuit.   10
non aliter stupui, quam qui Iovis ignibus ictus
    vivit et est vitae nescius ipse suae.
ut tamen hanc animi nubem dolor ipse removit,
    et tandem sensus convaluere mei,
alloquor extremum maestos abiturus amicos,   15
    qui modo de multis unus et alter erat.
uxor amans flentem flens acrius ipsa tenebat,
    imbre per indignas usque cadente genas.

Ovid, *Tristia* 1.3.1-18

Caesar, Caesaris – Caesar (i.e. Augustus, who had ordered Ovid into exile)
Ausonia, -ae – Italy
Iuppiter, Iovis – Jupiter

gutta, -ae, f – tear
torpeo, -ere – I am sluggish, numb
profugus, -i, m – fugitive

(a) Translate *cum subit … fuit* (lines 1-10).   [20]

(b) *non aliter … suae* (lines 11-12): what does the simile show us about Ovid's feelings? You should refer closely to the Latin and make two points.   [4]

(c) *ut tamen … mei* (lines 13-14): do you think at this point Ovid feels better or worse? Explain your answer.   [3]

(d) Which words in line 14 show that *sensus* must be plural? Explain your choice.   [2]

(e) *alloquor … alter erat* (lines 15-16) to whom does Ovid talk and when?   [3]

(f) *uxor … genas* (lines 17-18): how does Ovid emphasise his wife's grief? You should refer closely to the Latin and make two points.   [4]

(g) Write out and scan lines 7-8 (*nec spatium … nostra mora*).   [4]

14. Pious disobedience

Hypermnestra tells her husband how, unlike her sisters, she failed to obey her father's command that they should murder their husbands.

iamque cibo vinoque graves somnoque iacebant,
    securumque quies alta per Argos erat:
circum me gemitus morientum audire videbar –
    et tamen audieram, quodque verebar, erat.
sanguis abit, mentemque calor corpusque relinquit,   5
    inque novo iacui frigida facta toro,
ut leni Zephyro graciles vibrantur aristae,
    frigida populeas ut quatit aura comas,
aut sic, aut etiam tremui magis. ipse iacebas,
    quaeque tibi dederam vina, soporis erant.   10
excussere metum violenti iussa parentis;
    erigor et capio tela tremente manu.
non ego falsa loquar. ter acutum sustulit ensem,
    ter male sublato reccidit ense manus.
admovi iugulo – sine me tibi vera fateri –   15
    admovi iugulo tela paterna tuo;
sed timor et pietas crudelibus obstitit ausis
    castaque mandatum dextra refugit opus.

Ovid, *Heroides* 14.33-50

Argos – Argos (a town in the Peloponnese)
Zephyrus, -i – Zephyr (a warm west wind)

securus, -a, -um – undisturbed, tranquil
gemitus, -us, m – groan
audieram = audiveram
arista, -ae, f – ear of corn
populeus, -a, -um – of the poplar tree
excutio, -cutere, -cussi, -cussum – I shake out
recido, -cidere, -ccidi – I fall back, recoil
castus, -a, -um – chaste, pious

(a) Translate *iamque ... erant* (lines 1-10). [20]

(b) *excussere ... manu* (lines 11-12): what change of heart does Hypermnestra have and why? [2]

(c) *ter acutum ... manus* (lines 13-14):
    (i) what does Hypermnestra's hand do? [4]
    (ii) what effect do you think is created by having *manus* as the subject? [1]

(d) *excussere ... tuo* (lines 11-16): show how the language used here conveys Hypermnestra's horror at what she might have done. You should refer closely to the Latin and make three points. [6]

(e) *sed timor ... opus* (lines 17-18): explain why Hypermnestra did not murder her husband. [3]

(f) Write out and scan lines 17-18 (*sed timor ... opus*). [4]

15. Deification

Romulus is assumed into heaven during a storm. He later appears to Julius
Proculus and gives him instructions for his people.

est locus, antiqui Capreae dixere paludem:
  forte tuis illic, Romule, iura dabas.
sol fugit, et removent subeuntia nubila caelum,
  et gravis effusis decidit imber aquis.
hinc tonat, hinc missis abrumpitur ignibus aether: 5
  fit fuga, rex patriis astra petebat equis.
luctus erat, falsaeque patres in crimine caedis,
  haesissetque animis forsitan illa fides;
sed Proculus Longa veniebat Iulius Alba,
  lunaque fulgebat, nec facis usus erat,   10
cum subito motu saepes tremuere sinistrae:
  rettulit ille gradus, horrueruntque comae.
pulcher et humano maior trabeaque decorus
  Romulus in media visus adesse via
et dixisse simul 'prohibe lugere Quirites,   15
  nec violent lacrimis numina nostra suis:
tura ferant placentque novum pia turba Quirinum,
  et patrias artes militiamque colant.'
iussit et in tenues oculis evanuit auras;
  convocat hic populos iussaque verba refert.   20

Ovid, *Fasti* 2.491-510

Caprea, -ae – Caprea
Iulius Proculus, Iulii Proculi – Julius Proculus
Alba Longa, Albae Longae – Alba Longa
Quirites, Quiritium – Quirites (another name for citizens of Rome)
Quirinus, -i – Quirinus (Romulus' name when he became a god)

palus, paludis, f – marsh
nubila, -orum, n – clouds
luctus, -us, m – grief, mourning
patres, -um, m – here 'senators'
crimen, -inis, n – charge
fax, facis, f – torch
saepes, -is, f – hedgerow
trabea, -ae, f – royal robe
lugeo, lugere, luxi – I mourn
placo, -are – I appease

32

(a) *est locus ... dabas* (lines 1-2): what was happening at the Marsh of
    Caprea? [2]

(b) *sol ... aether* (lines 3-5): how is the storm made to seem dramatic?
    You should make three points and refer closely to the Latin used. [6]

(c) *luctus ... fides* (lines 7-8): how did the Romans react to Romulus'
    disappearance? [2]

(d) *sed Proculus ... sinistrae* (lines 9-11): what were the circumstances
    in which Romulus appeared to Julius Proculus? [5]

(e) Line 11: explain why *cum* is used here with an indicative (*tremuere*). [1]

(f) Translate *rettulit ... refert* (lines 12-20). [20]

(g) Write out and scan lines 19-20 (*iussit ... refert*). [4]

16. Different ambitions

*Ovid writes of his upbringing, and describes the different
ambitions that he and his brother had.*

protinus <u>excolimur</u> <u>teneri</u>, curaque parentis
    imus ad insignes urbis ab arte viros.
frater ad eloquium viridi tendebat ab <u>aevo</u>,
    fortia verbosi natus ad arma fori;
at mihi iam puero caelestia sacra placebant,   5
    inque suum furtim Musa trahebat opus.
saepe pater dixit 'studium quid inutile temptas?
    Maeonides nullas ipse reliquit opes.'
ı motus eram dictis, totoque Helicone relicto
    scribere temptabam verba soluta <u>modis</u>.   10
sponte sua carmen numeros veniebat ad aptos,
    et quod temptabam scribere versus erat.
interea tacito passu labentibus annis
    <u>liberior</u> fratri sumpta mihique toga est,
induiturque umeris cum lato purpura <u>clavo</u>,   15
    et studium nobis, quod fuit ante, manet.
iamque decem vitae frater <u>geminaverat</u> annos,
    cum perit, et coepi parte carere mei.

Ovid, *Tristia* 4.10.15-32

*Musa, -a*e – Muse (the poetic inspiration)
Maeonides, -ae – the man from Maeonia, i.e. Homer
Helicon, Heliconis – Mount Helicon (home to the Muses)

excolo, -colere, -colui, -cultum – I educate
tener, tenera, tenerum – tender, young
aevum, -i, n – age
modus, -i, m – rhythm, metre
liberior, liberioris – here: 'which brings more freedom'
clavus, -i, m – the (purple) stripe on the tunic (a broad stripe signified a
    senator)
gemino, -are – I double

(a) *protinus ... viros* (lines 1-2): how are the boys' teachers described? [2]
(b) *frater ... fori* (lines 3-4):
    (i) what career was Ovid's brother aiming for? [1]
    (ii) *fortia ... ad arma* is a metaphor: translate it and explain to what
    it refers. Do you think the metaphor is effective? [3]
(c) *at mihi ... opus* (lines 5-6): what do these lines tell us of Ovid's
    feelings about being a writer? You should quote, translate and
    comment on two details from the text. [4]
(d) *saepe ... opes* (lines 7-8): how do these lines make clear Ovid's
    father's disapproval? You should refer closely to the Latin and
    make three points. [6]
(e) Translate *motus ... mei* (lines 9-18). [20]
(f) Write out and scan lines 7-8 (*saepe ... opes*). [4]

17. A terrible storm

Ovid is at sea in a terrible storm.

terribilisque Notus iactat mea dicta, precesque
   ad quos mittuntur, non sinit ire deos.
ergo idem venti, ne causa laedar in una,
   velaque nescio quo votaque nostra ferunt.
me miserum, quanti montes volvuntur aquarum!   5
   iam iam tacturos sidera summa putes.
quantae diducto subsidunt aequore valles!
   iam iam tacturas Tartara nigra putes.
quocumque aspicio, nihil est, nisi pontus et aer,
   fluctibus hic tumidus, nubibus ille minax.   10
inter utrumque fremunt inmani murmure venti.
   nescit, cui domino pareat, unda maris.
nam modo purpureo vires capit Eurus ab ortu,
   nunc Zephyrus sero vespere missus adest,
nunc sicca gelidus Boreas bacchatur ab Arcto,   15
   nunc Notus adversa proelia fronte gerit.
rector in incerto est nec quid fugiatve petatve
   invenit: ambiguis ars stupet ipsa malis.

Ovid, *Tristia* 1.2.15-32

Notus, *-i* – the south wind
Tartara, *-orum* – Tartarus, i.e. the Underworld
Eurus, *-i* – the east wind
Zephyrus, *-i* – the west wind
Boreas, *-ae* – the north wind
Arctus, *-i* – the North

velum, *-i*, n – sail
aer, *aeris*, m – air
minax, *minacis* – threatening
serus, *-a*, *-um* – late
siccus, *-a*, *-um* – dry
bacchor, *-ari* – I rage, I run wild
rector, *-oris*, m – helmsman

17. A terrible storm

(a) *terribilisque … deos* (lines 1-2): what does the south wind do to
     Ovid's words and prayers?   [3]
(b) Translate *ergo … maris* (lines 3-12).   [20]
(c) *ergo … maris* (lines 3-12): how does the language used here
     emphasise the strength of the storm? You should refer in detail to
     the Latin and make three points.   [6]
(d) *nam modo … adest* (lines 13-14): give a literal translation of
     purpureo ab ortu and explain what you think Ovid means by it. [3]
(e) What do you think is the effect of the repetition of *nunc* in lines 14,
     15, 16?   [1]
(f) *rector … malis* (lines 17-18): what has happened to the helmsman? [3]
(g) Write out and scan lines 1-2 (*terribilisque … deos*).   [4]

18. An unwelcome lover

Apollo chases Daphne, with whom he has fallen in love.

spectat inornatos collo pendere <u>capillos</u>
et 'quid, si <u>comantur</u>?' ait. videt igne micantes
sideribus similes oculos, videt <u>oscula</u>, quae non
est vidisse satis; laudat digitosque manusque
bracchiaque et nudos media plus parte <u>lacertos</u>;   5
si qua latent, meliora putat. fugit ocior aura
illa levi neque ad haec revocantis verba resistit:
'nympha, precor, Penei, mane! non insequor hostis;
nympha, mane! sic <u>agna</u> lupum, sic cerva leonem,
sic aquilam penna fugiunt trepidante <u>columbae</u>,   10
hostes quaeque suos: amor est mihi causa sequendi!
me miserum! ne <u>prona</u> cadas indignave laedi
<u>crura</u> notent <u>sentes</u> et sim tibi causa doloris!
aspera, qua properas, loca sunt: moderatius, oro,
curre fugamque inhibe, moderatius insequar ipse.   15
cui placeas, inquire tamen: non incola montis,
non ego sum pastor, non hic armenta gregesque
horridus observo. nescis, <u>temeraria</u>, nescis,
quem fugias, <u>ideo</u>que fugis.'

Ovid, *Metamorphoses* 1.497-515

Peneis, -idis (vocative *Penei*) – daughter of Peneus

capillus, -i, m – hair
como, comere, compsi, comptum – I adorn
oscula, -orum, n pl – (here) lips
lacertus, -i, m – upper arm
agna, -ae, f – lamb
columba, -ae, f – dove
pronus, -a, -um – headlong
crus, cruris, n – leg
sentis, -is, m/f – thorn
temerarius, -a, -um – hasty, rash
ideo – for that reason

18. An unwelcome lover

(a) *spectat ... oculos* (lines 1-3): what are we told about Daphne's hair and eyes? [2]

(b) *videt oscula ... putat* (lines 3-6): identify two ways in which Ovid conveys Apollo's desire. You should make close reference to the Latin and explain your answer carefully. [4]

(c) *fugit ... resistit* (lines 6-7): how does Daphne react to Apollo's advances? [2]

(d) Translate *nympha ... observo* (lines 8-18). [20]

(e) *nympha ... observo* (lines 8-18): how does Apollo's speech emphasise his love for Daphne? You should refer closely to the Latin and make three points. [6]

(f) *nescis ... fugis* (lines 18-19): explain what Apollo means here. [2]

(g) Write out and scan lines 12-13 (*me miserum ... doloris*). [4]

19. Hopeless love

The staggeringly beautiful Narcissus has seen his own reflection in a pool and fallen in love.

'iste ego sum: sensi, nec me mea fallit imago;
uror amore mei: flammas moveoque feroque.
quid faciam? roger anne rogem? quid deinde rogabo?
quod cupio mecum est: inopem me copia fecit.
o utinam a nostro <u>secedere</u> corpore possem!   5
votum in amante novum, vellem, quod amamus, abesset.
iamque dolor vires adimit, nec tempora vitae
longa meae superant, primoque exstinguor in <u>aevo</u>.
nec mihi mors gravis est posituro morte dolores;
hic, qui diligitur, vellem <u>diuturnior</u> esset: 10
nunc duo concordes anima moriemur in una.'
dixit et ad faciem rediit male sanus eandem
et lacrimis turbavit aquas, obscuraque moto
reddita forma lacu est; quam cum vidisset abire,
quo refugis? remane nec me, crudelis, amantem   15
desere!' clamavit; 'liceat, quod tangere non est,
adspicere et misero praebere <u>alimenta</u> furori!'
dumque dolet, summa vestem deduxit ab ora
nudaque <u>marmoreis</u> percussit pectora palmis.

Ovid, *Metamorphoses* 3.463-81

secedo, -cedere, -cessi, -cessum – I go away from
aevum, -i, n – life-time
diuturnus, -a, -um – long-lasting
alimenta, -orum, n pl – food, fuel

(a) *iste … imago* (line 1): what has Narcissus understood?   [2]
(b) *uror … rogabo?* (lines 2-3): how is strength of Narcissus' passion
     made clear? You should refer closely to the Latin and make two
     points.   [4]
(c) *quod … fecit* (line 4): explain the problem that Narcissus has. [2]
(d) *o utinam … possem!* (line 5): what does Narcissus wish for and
     why?   [3]
(e) Translate *iamque … clamavit* (lines 7-16).   [20]
(f) *liceat … furori!* (lines 16-17): why does Narcissus ask to be
     allowed to look at his reflection?   [3]
(g) *nudaque … palmis* (line 19): what do you think is the effect of the
     adjective *marmoreis*?   [2]
(h) Write out and scan lines 3-4 (*quid faciam … fecit*).   [4]

20. Savage revenge

After boasting that her children were superior to those of the goddess Leto, Niobe has already lost her seven sons, slaughtered by Apollo and Artemis, and her husband by his suicide. She now has to watch as her seven daughters receive the same treatment as their brothers.

dixerat, et sonuit contento <u>nervus</u> ab arcu,
qui praeter Nioben unam conterruit omnes:
illa malo est audax. – stabant cum vestibus atris
ante <u>toros</u> fratrum demisso crine sorores;
e quibus una trahens haerentia <u>viscere</u> tela   5
inposito fratri moribunda <u>relanguit</u> ore;
altera solari miseram conata parentem
<u>conticuit</u> subito <u>duplicata</u>que vulnere caeco est.
haec frustra fugiens collabitur, illa sorori
inmoritur; latet haec, illam trepidare videres.   10
sexque datis leto diversaque vulnera passis
ultima restabat, quam toto corpore mater,
tota veste tegens 'unam minimamque relinque!
de multis minimam posco' clamavit 'et unam.'
dumque rogat, pro qua rogat, occidit: <u>orba</u> resedit   15
exanimes inter natos natasque virumque
<u>deriguit</u>que malis; nullos movet aura capillos,
in vultu color est sine sanguine, lumina maestis
stant inmota <u>genis</u>, nihil est in imagine vivum.

Ovid, *Metamorphoses* 6.286-305

nervus, *-i*, m – bowstring
torus, *-i*, m – bed, funeral bier
viscus, *-eris*, n – flesh
relanguesco, *-languescere*, *-langui* – I become faint
conticesco, *-ticescere*, *-ticui* – I become silent
duplico, *-are* – I bend double
orbus, *-a*, *-um* – bereft of children
derigesco, *-rigescere*, *-rigui* – I grow stiff
gena, *-ae*, f – cheek

(a) Translate *dixerat ... videres* (lines 1-10).   [20]
(b) *ultima ... unam* (lines 12-14):
    (i) which daughter is left?   [1]
    (ii) how does Ovid emphasise Niobe's desperation to save her?
    You should refer closely to the Latin and make three points.   [6]
(c) *dumque ... malis* (lines 15-17): what happens next?   [3]
(d) *deriguitque malis* (line 17): what do you think the atmosphere is
    here? Explain your answer.   [2]
(e) *nullos ... vivum* (lines 17-19): what are we told about Niobe's
    appearance?   [4]
(f) Write out and scan lines 7-8 (*altera ... est*).   [4]

21. Love at first sight

*Perseus, while flying through the air with his winged sandals, sees
the beautiful Andromeda, whom Poseidon had punished in
anger at her mother's boast that Andromeda was more
beautiful than Poseidon's daughters.*

quam simul ad duras religatam bracchia <u>cautes</u>
vidit Abantiades, nisi quod levis aura capillos
moverat et tepido <u>manabant</u> lumina fletu,
<u>marmoreum</u> ratus esset opus; trahit inscius ignes
et stupet et visae correptus imagine formae   5
paene suas <u>quatere</u> est oblitus in aere <u>pennas</u>.
ut stetit, 'o' dixit 'non istis digna catenis,
sed quibus inter se cupidi iunguntur amantes,
<u>pande</u> requirenti nomen terraeque tuumque,
et cur vincla geras.' primo silet illa nec audet   10
adpellare virum virgo, manibusque modestos
<u>celasset</u> vultus, si non religata fuisset;
lumina, quod potuit, lacrimis implevit obortis.
saepius instanti, sua ne <u>delicta</u> fateri
nolle videretur, nomen terraeque suumque,   15
quantaque maternae fuerit fiducia formae
indicat et nondum <u>memoratis</u> omnibus unda
insonuit, veniensque immenso <u>belua</u> ponto
inminet et latum sub pectore possidet aequor.

Ovid, *Metamorphoses* 4.672-690

Abantiades, -ae – Abas' descendant, i.e. Perseus

cautes, -is, f – rock
mano, -are – I drip
marmoreus, -a, -um – of marble
quatio, quatere, quassi, quassum – I shake, beat
pennae, -arum, f pl – wings
pando, pandere, pandi, pansum – I reveal
celasset = celavisset
delictum, -i, n – crime
memoro, -are – I recount
belua, -ae, f – beast, monster

44

(a) *quam ... cautes* (line 1): what has happened to Andromeda?   [2]
(b) *vidit ... fletu* (lines 2-3): how does Perseus know that Andromeda is
    alive?   [2]
(c) Give both a literal and an idiomatic translation of *trahit ignes*
    (line 4). Explain your answer.   [3]
(d) *et stupet ... amantes* (lines 5-8): what impression do these lines give
    us of Perseus? Explain your answer with close reference to the
    Latin, commenting on at least three details.   [6]
(e) *pande ... geras* (lines 9-10): what does Perseus ask Andromeda?   [3]
(f) Translate *primo ... aequor* (lines 10-19).   [20]
(g) Write out and scan lines 7-8 (*ut stetit ... amantes*).   [4]

22. A flood

Ovid paints an amusing picture of the topsy-turvy conditions when the world is flooded.

iamque mare et tellus nullum discrimen habebant:	
omnia pontus erat, <u>derant</u> quoque litora ponto.	
occupat hic collem, <u>cumba</u> sedet alter <u>adunca</u>	
et ducit <u>remos</u> illic, ubi nuper arabat:	
ille supra <u>segetes</u> aut mersae culmina villae	5
navigat, hic summa piscem deprendit in <u>ulmo</u>.	
figitur in viridi, si fors tulit, ancora <u>prato</u>,	
aut subiecta <u>terunt</u> curvae vineta carinae;	
et, modo qua graciles <u>gramen</u> <u>carpsere</u> <u>capellae</u>,	
nunc ibi deformes ponunt sua corpora <u>phocae</u>.	10
mirantur sub aqua <u>lucos</u> urbesque domosque	
Nereides, silvasque tenent delphines et altis	
incursant ramis agitataque robora pulsant.	
<u>nat</u> lupus inter oves, fulvos vehit unda leones,	
unda vehit tigres; nec vires fulminis <u>apro</u>,	15
<u>crura</u> nec ablato prosunt velocia cervo,	
quaesitisque diu terris, ubi sistere possit,	
in mare <u>lassatis</u> <u>volucris</u> <u>vaga</u> decidit alis.	
obruerat tumulos inmensa licentia ponti,	
pulsabantque novi montana <u>cacumina</u> fluctus.	20

Ovid, *Metamorphoses* 1.291-310

Nereis, -idis – a Nereid (a daughter of the sea god Nereus)

derant = deerant (desum)
cumba, -ae, f – small boat
aduncus, -a, -um – curved
remus, -i, m – oar
seges, -etis, f – crop, sown field
ulmus, -i, f – elm tree
pratum, -i, n – meadow
tero, terere, trivi, tritum – I rub, wear away
gramen, -inis, n – grass
carpo, carpere, carpsi, carptum – I pluck
capella, -ae, f – she-goat
phoca, -ae, f – seal
lucus, -i, m – sacred grove, wood

46

22. A flood

no, nare, navi – I swim
aper, apri, m – wild boar
crus, cruris, n – leg
lasso, -are – I make weary
volucris, volucris, f – bird
vagus, -a, -um – wandering
cacumen, -inis, n – top, summit

*

(a) Translate *iamque … phocae* (lines 1-10).   [20]
(b) *mirantur … Nereides* (lines 11-12): what causes the Nereids to be
     amazed?   [2]
(c) *silvasque … tigres* (lines 12-15): how is the topsy-turvy nature of
     the flood emphasised here? You should make two points and refer
     closely to the Latin used.   [4]
(d) *nec … cervo* (lines 15-16): what powers – useful before the flood –
     are ascribed here to the boar and the deer?   [2]
(e) *quaesitisque … alis* (lines 17-18): show how we are encouraged to
     feel pity for the bird. You should make two points and refer closely
     to the Latin used.   [4]
(f) *obruerat… fluctus* (lines 19-20): what aspect of the flood is being
     emphasised here, and how? You should refer closely to the Latin
     used.   [4]
(g) Write out and scan lines 1-2 (*iamque … ponto*).   [4]

23. Love lost for the second time

Orpheus, while bringing Eurydice back from the Underworld, forgets
the condition imposed upon him by Pluto and Persephone, and,
with dire consequences, looks back at his beloved.

iamque pedem referens casus evaserat omnes,
redditaque Eurydice superas veniebat ad auras
<u>pone</u> sequens (namque hanc dederat Proserpina legem),
cum subita incautum dementia cepit amantem,
ignoscenda quidem, scirent si ignoscere Manes.   5
restitit, Eurydicenque suam iam luce sub ipsa
immemor, heu, victusque animi respexit. ibi omnis
effusus labor atque immitis rupta tyranni
foedera, terque <u>fragor</u> stagnis auditus Avernis.
illa 'quis et me' inquit 'miseram et te perdidit, Orpheu,   10
quis tantus furor? en iterum crudelia retro
fata vocant, conditque natantia lumina somnus.
iamque vale: feror ingenti circumdata nocte
invalidasque tibi tendens, heu non tua, palmas.'
dixit et ex oculis subito, ceu fumus in auras   15
commixtus tenues, fugit diversa, neque illum
<u>prensantem</u> nequiquam umbras et multa volentem
dicere praeterea vidit; nec <u>portitor</u> Orci
amplius obiectam passus transire <u>paludem</u>.

Virgil, *Georgics* 4.485-503

Eurydice, -es – Eurydice
Proserpina, -ae – Proserpina, another name for Persephone, Queen of the
    Underworld
Manes, -ium – the Shades (spirits) of the dead
Avernus, -a, -um – belonging to Avernus, the lake at the entrance to the
    Underworld
Orpheus, -ei (voc. *Orpheu*) – Orpheus
Orcus, -i – Orcus, another name for the Underworld

pone – behind
fragor, -oris, m – crash, loud noise
prenso, -are – I clutch at
portitor, -oris, m – boatman
palus, paludis, f – swamp

(a) Translate *iamque ... Avernis* (lines 1-9). [20]

(b) *illa ... furor* (lines 10-11): how do Eurydice's words emphasise their shared love? You should make two points and refer closely to the Latin used. [4]

(c) *en iterum ... palmas* (lines 11-14): write out and translate four words which show death to be less pleasant than life. For each, explain your choice. [4]

(d) *dixit ... diversa* (lines 15-16): how does Eurydice disappear? [3]

(e) *neque ... vidit* (lines 16-18): what is Orpheus' reaction? [3]

(f) Line 19: *est* needs to be understood with *passus*. What verb is *passus* from and what is its meaning here? [2]

(g) Write out and scan lines 4-5 (*cum subita ... Manes*) [4]

24. Sea-snakes

In the tenth year of the Trojan War, the Greeks send Sinon – a skilful liar – to persuade the Trojans to take the wooden horse into their city. Just as he has finished his story, a terrifying omen appears from far out across the sea.

talibus insidiis periurique arte Sinonis
credita res, captique dolis lacrimisque coactis
quos neque Tydides nec Larissaeus Achilles,
non anni domuere decem, non mille carinae.
hic aliud maius miseris multoque tremendum   5
obicitur magis atque improvida pectora turbat.
Laocoon, ductus Neptuno sorte sacerdos,
sollemnes taurum ingentem mactabat ad aras.
ecce autem gemini a Tenedo tranquilla per alta
(horresco referens) immensis orbibus angues   10
incumbunt pelago pariterque ad litora tendunt;
pectora quorum inter fluctus arrecta iubaeque
sanguineae superant undas; pars cetera pontum
pone legit sinuatque immensa volumine terga.
fit sonitus spumante salo; iamque arva tenebant   15
ardentesque oculos suffecti sanguine et igni
sibila lambebant linguis vibrantibus ora.
diffugimus visu exsangues. illi agmine certo
Laocoonta petunt; et primum parva duorum
corpora natorum serpens amplexus uterque   20
implicat et miseros morsu depascitur artus.

Virgil, *Aeneid* 2.195-215

Sinon, Sinonis – Sinon
Tydides, -ae – Diomedes, the son of Tydeus
Larissaeus, -a, -um – of Larissa
Achilles, -is – Achilles
Laocoon, -ontis (acc. *Laocoonta*) – Laocoon
Neptunus, -i – Neptune
Tenedos, -i – Tenedos (an island near Troy)

domo, domare, domui, domitum – I conquer, subdue
sollemnis, -e – appointed
macto, -are – I kill
anguis -is, m/f – snake

50

incumbo, -cumbere, -cubui, -cubitum – I lean over, overhang
pelagus, -i, m – the sea
iuba, -ae, f – crest
lego, legere, legi, lectum – I move across
salum, -i, n – the sea
sufficio, -ficere, -feci, -fectum – I imbue, stain
depascor, -pasci – I feed off
artus, -us, m – limb

*

(a) *talibus ... carinae* (lines 1-4): what had the Trojans managed to
   withstand and what now has got the better of them?   [3]
(b) *hic aliud ... turbat* (lines 5-6): what atmosphere does Virgil create
   here? You should refer to two details from the Latin and explain
   their effect.   [4]
(c) *Laocoon ... sacerdos* (line 7): who was Laocoon?   [2]
(d) *sollemnes ... aras* (line 8): what was he doing?   [1]
(e) Translate *ecce ... ora* (lines 9-17).   [20]
(f) *ecce ... ora* (lines 9-17): show how Virgil makes the snakes seem
   truly hideous. You should refer closely to the Latin used and make
   two points.   [4]
(g) *illi ... artus* (lines 18-21): what do the snakes do to Laocoon's sons? [2]
(h) Write out and scan lines 16-17 (*ardentesque ... ora*).   [4]

2. Further Unseen Translations

1. Opposition to Caesar

*Pompey gathers support and the senate reacts to the threat to
the Roman republic that Caesar has created.*

misso ad vesperum senatu omnes, qui sunt eius ordinis, a Pompeio evocantur.
laudat promptos Pompeius atque in posterum confirmat, segniores castigat
atque incitat. multi undique ex veteribus Pompei exercitibus spe praemiorum
atque ordinum evocantur, multi ex duabus legionibus, quae sunt traditae a
Caesare, arcessuntur. completur urbs et ipsum comitium tribunis, centurionibus, evocatis. omnes amici consulum, necessarii Pompei atque eorum,
qui veteres inimicitias cum Caesare gerebant, in senatum coguntur; quorum
vocibus et concursu terrentur infirmiores, dubii confirmantur, plerisque vero
libere decernendi potestas eripitur. pollicetur L. Piso censor sese iturum ad
Caesarem, item L. Roscius praetor, qui de his rebus eum doceant: sex dies ad
eam rem conficiendam spatii postulant. dicuntur etiam ab nonnullis senten-
tiae, ut legati ad Caesarem mittantur, qui voluntatem senatus ei proponant.

omnibus his resistitur, omnibusque oratio consulis, Scipionis, Catonis opponi-
tur. Catonem veteres inimicitiae Caesaris incitant et dolor repulsae.

Caesar, *De Bello Civili* 1.3-4

L. Piso, L. Pisonis – Lucius Piso
L. Roscius, L. Roscii – Lucius Roscius
Scipio, Scipionis – Scipio
Cato, Catonis – Cato

mitto, mittere, misi, missum – (here) I dismiss
segnis, -e – slow, sluggish
comitium, -i, n – comitium (in Rome, the area at the end of the forum where
the people assembled for public decision making)
decerno, decernere, decrevi, decretum – I decide
spatium, -i, n – space, interval (here, genitive after *sex dies*)
repulsa, -ae, f – defeat, rejection

2. Tall Poppies

Tarquinius Superbus, king of Rome, has been at war with the Volscians. During a lull in hostilities his son, Sextus Tarquinius, pretending to be a deserter, gets himself installed as military commander at Gabii, a Volscian town. When he is satisfied that he has established a sufficient power-base, he consults his father about what to do next.

Sextus igitur, cum sensim ad bellum renovandum primores Gabinorum incitaret, ipse cum promptissimis iuvenum praedatum atque in expeditiones iret et dictis factisque omnibus ad fallendum instructis vana adcresceret fides, dux postremo belli legitur. ibi cum, inscia multitudine quid ageretur, proelia parva inter Romam Gabiosque fierent quibus plerumque Gabina res superior esset, tum summi infimique Gabinorum Sex. Tarquinium dono deum sibi missum ducem credebant. apud milites vero obeundo pericula ac labores pariter, praedam munifice largiendo tanta caritate erat ut non pater Tarquinius potentior Romae quam filius Gabiis esset. itaque postquam satis virium conlectum ad omnes conatus videbat, tum ex suis unum sciscitatum Romam ad patrem mittit quidnam se facere vellet, cum ut omnia unus publice Gabiis posset ei di dedissent. huic nuntio, quia, credo, dubiae fidei videbatur, nihil voce responsum est; rex velut deliberabundus in hortum aedium transit sequente nuntio filii; ibi inambulans tacitus summa papaverum capita dicitur baculo decussisse. interrogando exspectandoque responsum nuntius fessus, ut re imperfecta, redit Gabios; quae dixerit ipse quaeque viderit refert; seu ira seu odio seu superbia insita ingenio nullam eum vocem emisisse. Sexto ubi quid vellet parens quidve praeciperet tacitis ambagibus patuit, primores civitatis sine mora interemit. multi palam, quidam clam interfecti.

Livy 1.54

Sextus Tarquinius, Sexti Tarquinii – Sextus Tarquinius
Gabini, -orum – the Gabini
Gabii, -orum – Gabii (an ancient city in Latium)

sensim – gradually
praedor, -ari – I plunder
expeditio, -onis, f – (here) foray (for raiding)
largior, -iri – I give generously
caritas, -atis, f – affection, esteem
sciscitor, -ari – I enquire
unus, -a, -um – (here) alone
deliberabundus, -a, -um – deliberating
papaver, papaveris, n – poppy
baculum, -i, n – staff
decutio, -cutere, -cussi, -cussum – I knock off
ambages, ambagum, f pl – riddles
pateo, -ere – I am revealed

3. Against Antony

Cicero inveighs against Antony.

reliquum est, Quirites, ut vos in ista sententia, quam prae vobis fertis, persev-
eretis. faciam igitur, ut imperatores instructa acie solent, quamquam paratissi-
mos milites ad proeliandum videant, ut eos tamen adhortentur. non est vobis,
Quirites, cum eo hoste certamen, cum quo aliqua pacis condicio esse possit.
neque enim ille servitutem vestram ut antea, sed iam iratus sanguinem concu-
pivit. nullus ei ludus videtur esse iucundior quam cruor, quam caedes, quam
ante oculos trucidatio civium. non est vobis res, Quirites, cum scelerato
homine ac nefario, sed cum immani taetraque belua, quae quoniam in foveam
incidit, obruatur. si enim illinc emerserit, nullius supplicii crudelitas erit
recusanda. sed tenetur, premitur, urgetur nunc iis copiis, quas iam habemus,
mox iis, quas paucis diebus novi consules comparabunt. incumbite in causam,
Quirites, ut facitis. numquam maior consensus vester in ulla causa fuit,
numquam tam vehementer cum senatu consociati fuistis. nec mirum; agitur
enim, non qua condicione victuri, sed victurine simus an cum supplicio
ignominiaque perituri.

Cicero, *Philippic* 4.5.11

Quirites, Quiritium – Quirites (another name for citizens of Rome)

concupisco, concupiscere, concupivi, concupitum – I desire eagerly
taeter, taetra, taetrum – foul, hideous
fovea, -ae, f – pit (for catching animals)
obruo, -ruere, -rui, -rutum – I cover over, bury
recuso, -are – I reject
incumbo, -cumbere, -cubui, -cubitum – I apply myself to

4. Drawings in the sand

The sea-nymph, Calypso, attempts to detain Ulysses with questions about the Trojan War; he replies with an illustrated account of his raid on the camp of Rhesus.

non formosus erat, sed erat <u>facundus</u> Ulixes,
    et tamen aequoreas torsit amore deas.
a quotiens illum doluit <u>properare</u> Calypso,
    remigioque aptas esse negavit aquas!
haec Troiae casus iterumque iterumque rogabat: 5
    ille referre aliter saepe solebat idem.
litore constiterant: illic quoque pulchra Calypso
    <u>exigit</u> Odrysii fata cruenta ducis.
ille levi <u>virga</u> (virgam nam forte tenebat)
    quod rogat, in <u>spisso</u> <u>litore</u> pingit opus.   10
'haec' inquit 'Troia est' (muros in litore fecit):
    'hic tibi sit Simois; haec mea castra puta.
illic Sithonii fuerant tentoria Rhesi:
    hac ego sum captis nocte revectus equis.'
pluraque pingebat, subitus cum Pergama fluctus   15
    abstulit et Rhesi cum duce castra suo.
tum dea 'quas' inquit 'fidas tibi credis ituro,
    <u>perdiderint</u> undae nomina quanta vides?'

Ovid, *Ars Amatoria* 2.122-39

Ulixes, -is – Ulysses
Calypso, -us – Calypso
Odrysius, -a, -um – Odrysian (= Thracian)
Simois, Simoentis – Simois (a stream in Troy)
Sithonius, -a, -um – Sithonian (= Thracian)
Rhesus, -i – Rhesus
Pergama, -orum – Pergama (= Troy)

facundus, -a, -um – eloquent
propero, -are – (here) I hurry on my way
exigo, -igere, -egi, -actum – I demand
virga, -ae, f – stick
spissus, -a, -um – thick
litus, litoris, n – (here) sand
perdo, perdere, perdidi, perditum – I destroy

5. Joyous love

Propertius is delighted that he has won Cynthia's heart.

hic erit! hic <u>iurata</u> manet! rumpantur <u>iniqui</u>!
   vicimus: assiduas non tulit illa preces.
falsa licet cupidus deponat gaudia <u>livor</u>:
   <u>destitit</u> ire novas Cynthia nostra vias.
illi carus ego et per me carissima Roma   5
   dicitur, et sine me dulcia regna negat.
illa vel angusto mecum requiescere lecto
   et quocumque modo maluit esse mea,
quam sibi <u>dotatae</u> regnum vetus Hippodamiae,
   et quas Elis opes apta <u>pararat</u> equis.   10
quamvis magna daret, quamvis maiora daturus,
   non tamen illa meos fugit avara <u>sinus</u>.
hanc ego non auro, non Indis flectere <u>conchis</u>,
   sed potui blandi carminis <u>obsequio</u>.
sunt igitur Musae, neque amanti tardus Apollo,   15
   quis ego <u>fretus</u> amo: Cynthia <u>rara</u> <u>meast</u>!
nunc mihi summa licet contingere sidera <u>plantis</u>:
   sive dies seu nox venerit, illa meast!
nec mihi rivalis certos subducet amores:
   ista meam <u>norit</u> gloria <u>canitiem</u>.   20

Propertius 1.8B.27-46

Hippodamia, -ae – Hippodamia
Elis, *-idis* – Elis

iuro, -ari – I swear (*iuratus* – having sworn)
iniqui, -orum, m pl – enemies
livor, -oris, m – envy
desisto, -sistere, -stiti, -stitum + inf – I cease
dotatus, -a, -um – richly dowered
pararat = paraverat
sinus, -us, m – embrace
concha, -ae, f – pearl
obsequium, -i, n – compliance, (here) gift
fretus, -a, -um + abl – relying upon
rarus, -a, -um – exquisite
meast = mea est
planta, -ae, f – (here) finger-tips
norit = noverit
canities, -ei, f – old age

6. Foul murder

En route to Italy, Aeneas lands in Thrace and encounters the spirit of Priam's youngest son Polydorus, who had been sent there by his father with great quantities of gold when it seemed likely that Troy would fall to the Greeks. Here, Aeneas describes what happened and tells how he performed new funeral rites for Polydorus.

hunc Polydorum auri quondam cum pondere magno
infelix Priamus furtim mandarat alendum
Threicio regi, cum iam diffideret armis
Dardaniae cingique urbem obsidione videret.
ille, ut opes fractae Teucrum et Fortuna recessit,   5
res Agamemnonias victriciaque arma secutus
fas omne abrumpit: Polydorum obtruncat, et auro
vi potitur. quid non mortalia pectora cogis,
auri sacra fames! postquam pavor ossa reliquit,
delectos populi ad proceres primumque parentem   10
monstra deum refero, et quae sit sententia posco.
omnibus idem animus, scelerata excedere terra,
linqui pollutum hospitium et dare classibus Austros.
ergo instauramus Polydoro funus, et ingens
aggeritur tumulo tellus; stant Manibus arae   15
caeruleis maestae vittis atraque cupresso,
et circum Iliades crinem de more solutae;
inferimus tepido spumantia cymbia lacte
sanguinis et sacri pateras, animamque sepulcro
condimus et magna supremum voce ciemus.   20

Virgil, *Aeneid* 3.49-6

64

Threicius, -a, -um – Thracian
Dardania, -ae – Dardania (= Troy)
Teucri, -orum – Trojans
Teucrum = Teucrorum
Agamemnonius, -a, -um – of Agamemnon
Auster, Austri – south wind
Ilias, Iliadis – Trojan woman

mandarat = *mandaverat*
alo, alere, alui, alitum – I rear, bring up
cingo, cingere, cinxi, cinctum – I encircle
sacer, sacra, sacrum – (here) cursed
proceres, -um, m pl – leaders
monstrum, -i, n – portent
instauro, -are – I make / do afresh, renew
aggero, -gerere, -gessi, -gestum – I heap up
vitta, -ae, f – ribbon
cupressus, -i, f – cypress wood
cymbium, -i, n – small cup
lac, lactis, n – milk
patera, -ae, f – shallow bowl
supremum cieo, ciere, civi, citum – I call upon for the last time

3. Prose Compositions

Latin Composition 1

Translate into Latin:

On receipt of this news[1], Caesar, when he had called together all his troops, went forward[2] to the tribunal and made a speech as follows: 'We have now, soldiers, discovered from scouts the plans of the enemy. A few, because they are afraid to fight, have retreated to nearby towns and villages; the majority, however, thinking[3] that they can easily defeat us, weakened[4] as we are by many disasters, have hidden themselves in these woods, and intend[5] to come out tomorrow in order to join battle with us at dawn. Since this is so[6], my advice to you now is to return to your tents and prepare dinner; for in the morning we must fight with all our might[7] to save our fatherland.' Encouraged by these words[8], the troops began to shout in a loud voice. Soon some were preparing food, whilst others were piling up[9] their arms. A few, however, were so frightened that after a brief conference with each other[10] they decided to take to flight. In the middle of the night, therefore, they stealthily[11] left the camp and headed for their homes.

Notes

1. 'on receipt of this news': use ablative absolute here.
2. 'went forward': use perfect participle of *progredior*, and then omit the 'and' later in the sentence.
3. 'thinking': *ratus, -a, -um.*
4. 'weakened': use *fractus, -a, -um.*
5. 'I intend': *in animo habeo* + infinitive.
6. = *quae cum ita sint.*
7. 'with all our might': *summa vi.*
8. There is an opportunity here to use a connecting relative.
9. 'I pile up': *congero, -ere, -gessi, -gestum.*
10. 'after a brief conference with each other' = 'having briefly spoken together (*colloquor*) amongst themselves'.
11. 'stealthily': *furtim.*

Latin Composition 2

Translate into Latin:

Scipio Nasica[1], a very famous senator, once came to visit[2] his friend, the poet Ennius, in order to consult him on a matter of very great importance[3]. However, when he had arrived at his villa and had enquired for his friend at the front door[4], the housemaid told him that her master was not at home. Scipio, suspecting[5] that she was lying, and that she had given this reply[6] at her master's bidding, angrily turned on his heel[7] and quickly went away without saying anything more[8]. A few days later Ennius, because he was afraid that this deception had cost him Scipio's friendship[9], decided to pay him a visit[10]. When he had knocked at the door[11], Scipio himself shouted out loudly that he was not at home, and sternly instructed his friend to depart. Hearing this[12], Ennius said, 'Don't try to fool me, my friend. Do I not recognise your voice?' But Scipio replied that he was an impudent fellow[13]. 'For,' he said, 'if I believed your maidservant, surely you ought to believe me myself?'

Notes

1. = *Scipio* (*-ionis*, m) *Nasica* (*-ae*, m).
2. 'I come to visit': *venio, -ire, veni, ventum ad* + accusative.
3. 'a matter of very great importance' = 'a very important matter'.
4. 'front door': *ostium, -ii*, n. For 'at' use *ab* + ablative.
5. 'suspecting': use perfect participle of *suspicor*, i.e. *suspicatus, -a, -um*.
6. 'had given this reply' = 'had replied this'.
7. 'I turn on my heel': *me converto, -ere, converti, conversum*.
8. 'without saying anything more' = 'not having said more things'.
9. 'that this deception had cost him Scipio's friendship' = 'that by this deception he had lost his friend'.
10. 'pay him a visit' = 'visit (*viso, -ere, visi, visum*) him'.
11. 'I knock at the door': *ianuam pulso* (1).
12. An opportunity here for a connecting relative.
13. 'fellow': *homo, -inis*, m.

Latin Composition 3

(based on Part 1, Unseen No 9, Livy 1.26)

Translate into Latin:

Horatius[1] had defeated and killed the three Curiatii[2] and was now leading his victorious army back to Rome. The country had been saved by this victory, and all the citizens were there to greet him joyfully as he carried the spoils[3] of war into the city. As he entered through the Porta Capena he was met by his maiden sister[4], who had secretly been betrothed[5] to one of those whom her brother had killed. Recognising on his shoulders a cloak[6] which she herself had made, she was overcome with grief and called upon her fiancé[7] by name. At this[8] Horatius became so angry that he drew his sword and ran the girl through[9] with it on the spot[10]. This deed seemed terrible to both senators and people, and the young man was arrested and brought to trial. However, when his father declared that his daughter had paid a fair penalty[11] for her treachery, and begged the citizens not to make him totally childless[12], the judges, moved by the old man's tears, acquitted[13] Horatius and praised his valour.

Notes

1. = *Horatius, -ii*, m.
2. = *Curiatii, -orum*, m pl.
3. 'spoils': *spolia, -orum*, n pl.
4. 'he was met by': turn this to the active, i.e. 'his maiden sister met (*obviam eo, ire, ivi, itum* + dative) him'.
5. 'I betroth': *despondeo, -ere, -spondi, -sponsum*.
6. 'cloak': *paludamentum, -i*, n.
7. 'fiancé': *sponsus, -i*, m.
8. 'At this': use ablative absolute = 'which thing (connecting relative) having been heard'.
9. 'I run through': *confodio, -ere, -fodi, -fossum*.
10. 'on the spot': *ilico*.
11. 'I pay the penalty': *poenas do, dare, dedi, datum*.
12. 'childless': *orbus, -a, -um* (+ ablative, i.e. *orbus liberis*).
13. 'I acquit': *absolvo, -ere, -solvi, -solutum*.

Latin Composition 4

(based on Part 1, Unseen No 6, Livy 1.56)

Translate into Latin:

Tarquin the Proud[1], a man neither just nor dear to his people, was the last king of Rome[2]. Once, during his reign[3], a snake slithered out from a wooden column and struck such great panic into the hearts of all present, that the king decided to send two of his sons to Delphi[4], to ask[5] the god what should be done[6]. Further, because at that time this journey was very dangerous, he gave them as a companion his sister's son, Lucius[7] Junius Brutus, a clever young man, but one who always pretended to be stupid, in order to avoid execution at the hands of his uncle[8].

When they had heard Apollo's reply, the king's sons asked the god which[9] of the two of them would be king at Rome. Immediately he replied that the first to give[10] a kiss to his mother would have the supreme power there. Titus and Arruns then ordered Brutus not to reveal this to anyone, but he, realising the god's true meaning[11], fell down and kissed[12] the earth, the common mother of all mankind.

Notes

1. = *Tarquinius Superbus, Tarquinii Superbi*, m.
2. 'of Rome' = 'of the Romans'.
3. 'during his reign' = 'when he was reigning' – I reign = *regno* (1).
4. 'to Delphi': n.b. name of a town.
5. 'to ask': use relative here, i.e. *qui* + subjunctive.
6. 'should be done': use gerundive.
7. Lucius: use standard abbreviation = *L.*
8. 'in order ... uncle' = 'lest he be killed by his uncle' – uncle = *avunculus, -i*, m.
9. 'which' (of two): *uter, -tra, -trum.*
10. 'the first to give' = 'he who first gave'; use pluperfect subjunctive here, to represent in oratio obliqua the future perfect of direct speech.
11. 'the god's true meaning' = 'what the god really (*re vera*) meant'.
12. I kiss: *osculor* (1).

Latin Composition 5

Translate into Latin:

When Marius had been thrown into prison[1] at Minturnae, a public slave of German nationality[2] was sent to kill him. Marius, seeing him coming with drawn[3] sword, said, 'Will you, a slave, kill the general Gaius Marius?'[4] On hearing these words the slave threw away his sword and rushed from the prison crying that he was afraid to kill such a great man who had defeated[5] so many enemies of the Roman people. Then the people of Minturnae[6], believing[7] that the slave had been inspired with fear by the gods[8], released Marius from custody and, after giving him clothing and journey-money[9], prepared a ship for him to travel to Africa[10]. While he was staying there among the Carthaginians, the lictor of the praetor Sextius who was then governor[11] of Africa came and gave him orders to leave the province without delay on the praetor's instructions. For a long time Marius held his peace, as if he had heard nothing; but when the lictor at last asked him if he wanted any message taken back, he said[12], 'Say that you have seen Gaius Marius sitting among the ruins of Carthage.'

Notes

1. 'I throw into prison': *in vincula conicio, -ere, conieci, coniectum.*
2. 'of German nationality' = 'a German by birth'.
3. 'I draw (a sword): (*gladium*) *stringo, -ere, strinxi, strictum.*
4. 'Will you ... Marius?': this whole question should probably be treated as a question expecting the answer 'no', i.e. *num.*
5. 'who had defeated': this subordinate clause in indirect speech will have its verb in the subjunctive.
6. = *Minturnenses, -ium,* m pl.
7. This participial clause is in essence causal, a good opportunity for using *quippe qui* + subjunctive.
8. 'that the slave ... gods' = 'that fear had been cast upon (*inicio*) the slave by the gods'.
9. 'journey-money': *viaticum, -i,* n.
10. 'for him to travel to Africa' : final relative, i.e. 'in which he might travel'.
11. 'I am governor of': *obtineo* (2) + accusative.
12. 'but when ... he said' = 'but to the lictor asking ... he said'.

Latin Composition 6

Translate into Latin:

Once Hostius had fallen, the Roman troops immediately began to give ground[1], and Romulus himself was driven by the throng of fleeing soldiers to the old gate of the Palatine[2]. There, raising his weapons towards the sky, 'Jupiter,' he cried[3], 'it was on the instruction of your birds that[4] I laid the first foundations[5] of the city here on the Palatine; the Sabines have now taken the citadel and hold it; from there armed men are so quickly advancing across the valley that they will soon be upon us. I beg you[6], father of men and gods[7], compel the enemy to depart from here; restore their customary courage to the Romans and stop[8] their flight; for my part[9] I promise that, if you come to our aid[10], I will build you a temple here to be a memorial[11] to our descendants that the city was saved by your help.' After making this prayer, the king immediately seemed to believe that the god had heard him. 'Romans,' he said, 'Jupiter greatest and best bids you stop here and renew the fight.' Hearing these words[12], the Romans, as if[13] bidden by a divine voice, obeyed their leader; and Romulus, with a band of the fiercest young men, made a charge and drove back the enemy.

Notes

1. 'I give ground': *loco cedo, cedere, cessi, cessum.*
2. 'the Palatine': *Palatium, -ii*, n.
3. 'he cried': whatever the English says, it is best with direct speech to use *inquit* (or *ait*) and (here) to get in the extra idea by using a phrase like 'in a loud voice'.
4. 'it was … that …': translate using perfect participle passive = 'ordered by your birds I …'.
5. 'I lay foundations': *fundamenta pono, -ere, posui, positum* or *iacio, -ere, ieci, iactum.*
6. 'I beg you': at least one way to deal with this is to introduce the imperative by *at tu* (lit. 'but you').
7. Note that the genitive plural of *deus* is often contracted from *deorum* to *deum.*
8. 'stop': use *sisto, -ere, stiti, statum.*
9. 'for my part': *equidem.*
10. 'I come to the aid of': *subvenio, -ire, -veni, -ventum* + dative. Note that in this conditional clause in Oratio Obliqua the verb will be in the perfect subjunctive.
11. 'to be a memorial' = 'that it might be a memorial': use a final relative here (i.e. a purpose clause introduced by a relative pronoun).
12. Use a connecting relative here.
13. *quasi* may be followed by a participle, just like 'as if' in English.

Latin Composition 7

Translate into Latin:

When Diviciacus[1] had made this speech, all who were present began, with copious[2] tears, to ask Caesar for help. He, however, noticed that alone of them all the Sequani[3] were doing none of the things which the others were doing[4], but were sadly[5] gazing at the ground with bowed heads[6]. Wondering[7] what the reason for this was, he asked them why they seemed so unhappy. They made no reply[8], but remained sad and silent as before. If Caesar had asked them this question a second time, perhaps they would have given a reply; but, before there was a chance of that[9], Diviciacus himself replied as follows: the Sequani[10] were more unhappy than all the rest, for they alone dared neither to make a complaint[11] nor to beg for help, but always dreaded the cruelty of Ariovistus, even in his absence[12], just as if he were present face to face[13]. On learning this, Caesar comforted the Gauls[14] with kind words and promised to attend to the matter[15].

Notes

1. = *Diviciacus, -i*, m.
2. 'copious' = 'many'.
3. = *Sequani, -orum*, m pl.
4. 'were doing': the verb in this subordinate clause in indirect speech will be in the subjunctive.
5. 'sadly': best to use an adjective here rather than an adverb.
6. = *capite demisso.*
7. 'wondering': use perfect participle of *miror*.
8. 'made no reply = 'replied nothing'.
9. 'before … that' = 'before this could happen': *priusquam* + subjunctive.
10. 'the Sequani…face to face': the whole of this section is in indirect speech.
11. 'make a complaint' = 'complain'.
12. 'in his absence': use *absens* agreeing with *Ariovistus* = 'of Ariovistus even (being) absent'.
13. 'face to face': use the adverb *coram*.
14. 'comforted the Gauls' = 'strengthened (*confirmo*) the minds of the Gauls'.
15. 'to attend to the matter' = either 'that he would care for (*curo*) the matter', or 'that that matter would be for a care (*curae* = predicative dative) to him'.

Latin Composition 8

(based on Part 2, Unseen No 2, Livy 1.54)

Translate into Latin:

But when the Romans were already at war with the Volscians, Sextus Tarquinius, the king's son, took himself off[1] to a neighbouring Volscian town called Gabii, on pretence of being[2] an enemy of the Roman people. There he so often helped the Gabini both by what he said and by what he did[3], that in a short time they began to believe that the gods had sent them this young man as their leader in war. As soon as he had gained enough influence among them, he sent one of his own men to Rome, to find out what his father wanted him to do. However, when the messenger arrived there and was brought into the palace, the king gave no verbal reply[4], but immediately went out into his garden. There, while walking in silence among the flowers, he cut off the tallest[5] poppy-heads with his sword, and ordered the messenger to go back to his son. He, returning[6] to Gabii without delay, reported to the son what had happened. The king, he declared[7], whether out of anger or arrogance, had given no reply. Sextus, however, was easily able to understand his father's meaning, and, arresting all the leading citizens of Gabii, put them to death.

Notes

1. 'I take myself off': *me confero, -ferre, -tuli, -latum.*
2. 'on pretence of being ...' = 'as if he were ...', or 'pretending that he was ...'.
3. 'both by what he said and what he did' = 'by both words and deeds'.
4. 'gave no verbal reply' = 'replied nothing by word/voice'.
5. 'tallest': use *summus, -a, -um.*
6. NB: not a present participle here.
7. There is no need here to express the verb of saying. Simply put a colon after 'what had happened', and treat the next section as Oratio Obliqua (accusative plus infinitive). This will work well, even though the indirect speech began with an indirect question rather than an indirect statement.

Latin Composition 9

Translate into Latin:

When, amid the general panic[1], Curio[2] realised the extent[3] of the enemy army, he immediately gave orders to his troops to head for[4] the nearby hills. But cavalrymen, sent ahead by the enemy commander, had already taken possession of[5] these too. Then indeed our men plumbed the very depths of despair[6], and many were slaughtered by the enemy while[7] they attempted to flee. If Curio himself had been willing to take to flight[8], he could[9] easily have escaped to safety. He declared, however, that having lost the army which he had received[10] from Caesar he would never return into his presence[11]; and so he fell fighting bravely in battle. A few cavalry, who on the previous day had stayed behind in the town to refresh their horses, at last got safely[12] back to camp; but the rest, and all the infantry, were slaughtered to the last man[13].

Notes

1. 'amid the general panic': use an ablative absolute = 'all having been terrified'.
2. = *Curio, -ionis*, m. It's often a good idea, if the subject of a subordinate clause is the same as the subject of the main clause, to extract it and put it at the very beginning: e.g. 'Curio, when …, immediately ordered … etc.'.
3. 'the extent of': use an indirect question = 'how big the army was'.
4. 'I head for': *peto, -ere, -ivi, -itum.*
5. 'I take possession of': *occupo* (1).
6. 'I plumb the (very) depths of despair': *ad summam desperationem pervenio, -ire, -veni, -ventum.*
7. 'while': use either a present participle, or *dum* with the present indicative.
8. 'I take to flight': *me fugae mando* (1), *me in fugam do, dare, dedi, datum* (*confero* or *conicio* also possible).
9. When *possum* or *debeo* is the verb in the apodosis (main clause) of an Unreal Past Condition, it usually remains in the Perfect Indicative, rather than going into the Pluperfect Subjunctive.
10. The verb will be in the subjunctive in this subordinate clause in Indirect Speech.
11. 'presence': use *conspectus, -us*, m.
12. 'safely': use adjective here, agreeing with the subject, rather than adverb.
13. 'to the last man': *ad unum.*

Latin Composition 10

Translate into Latin:

In the meantime, in order not to go hungry[1], the Greeks were compelled to slaughter their beasts of burden; then, gathering up arrows, shields and other relics of battle which they found not far from the camp, they made a fire and began to cook their food. Round about[2] midday[3] some messengers arrived from the king of Persia, accompanied by Phalinus[4] the Zacynthian, who was highly influential with[5] Tissaphernes on account of his skill in military matters. Their mission was[6] to instruct the Greeks to lay down their arms at once and throw themselves on the king's mercy[7]. Scarcely had they delivered their instruction when[8] Clearchus, the Greek leader, was called away to inspect some sacrificial victims[9]. So, delaying only to observe that it was not usual for conquerors[10] to hand over their arms, he ordered his colleagues to give such an answer as seemed most appropriate to them and immediately departed.

Notes

1. 'in order not to go hungry' = either 'in order not to suffer hunger', or 'lest they should lack (*careo* (2) + ablative) food'.
2. 'round about': *circa* + accusative.
3. = *meridies, -ei*, m.
4. 'accompanied by': use an ablative absolute with a present participle = 'with Phalinus accompanying' (*comitor, -ari*).
5. 'was highly influential with' = 'was of great influence (ablative of description, *auctoritas, -atis*, f) with (*apud* + accusative), or use *polleo* (2) *apud* + accusative.
6. 'their mission was to' = 'they had been ordered to'.
7. 'to throw themselves on the king's mercy': at its simplest this need be no more than 'to hand themselves over to the king' (*se regi tradere*); slightly more complex are (i) *in fidem regis se tradere* and (ii) *arbitrio regis se submittere*.
8. *cum* + perfect indicative here, the so-called '*cum inversum*' or 'inverted *cum*'.
9. = *victima, -ae*, f.
10. 'that it was not usual for conquerors …' = 'that conquerors were not accustomed …'.

Latin Composition 11

Translate into Latin:

As soon as they had crossed the threshold[1], the conspirators barred[2] the doors, fell upon Philip as he lay in bed, and proceeded[3] to bind him in chains. Immediately an uproar arose in the palace, so loud indeed that it could be heard even outside. And here one may easily understand[4] just how unpopular absolute power is, and how unhappy the life of those who prefer to be feared than to be loved; for, while the conspirators, who happened to be unarmed[5], were demanding a weapon with which to finish the king off, his bodyguards[6], had they been well-disposed[7] to him, might perhaps have broken down the doors and tried to save him. No one, however, came to his aid, and in the meantime a certain Thracian called Seuthes handed a small dagger[8] through the window; with this Philip was speedily despatched.

Notes

1. 'I cross the threshold': *limen intro* (1).
2. 'I bar': *obsero* (1).
3. 'proceeded to': no need to express this in Latin; just say 'bound him in chains'.
4. 'one may easily understand' = 'it can easily be understood'.
5. 'happened to be unarmed' = 'by chance were unarmed'.
6. 'bodyguards': *stipatores, -um*, m.
7. 'well-disposed': *benevolus, -a, -um.*
8. 'Thracian': *Thrax, -acis*, m.
9. 'dagger': *pugio, -onis*, m.

Latin Composition 12

Translate into Latin:

And yet there are some people in this body[1], senators[2], of the sort[3] who either fail to see or do not wish to see what is threatening the state, who have nourished Catiline's hopes with their mild views and strengthened his conspiracy in its infancy[4] by not believing in it. Under their[5] influence many citizens, not just the wicked, but also the ignorant, would certainly have said that I acted with tyrannical cruelty[6], had I recently imposed upon Catiline the punishment[7] which he deserves[8]. As it is[9], I am confident that, if he joins Manlius' forces within a few days, no one will be so foolish as not to see that a conspiracy has been formed, no one so wicked as not to admit it. For if we execute Catiline alone, senators, I am quite sure that this disease which afflicts our country[10] can be checked for a short time, but not suppressed for ever[11]; but if he exiles[12] himself and takes away all his friends with him, it is not only this pestilence of the state which will be extinguished and destroyed, but also the root and seed of all evil.

Notes

1. 'body': use *ordo, -inis*, m.
2. 'senators': best to use *patres* or *patres conscripti*.
3. 'of the sort who': the generic sense will best be given in Latin here by using *qui* + subjunctive.
4. 'in its infancy': use the present participle of *nascor* here, in agreement with *coniuratio*.
5. An opportunity for a connecting relative here.
6. 'with tyrannical cruelty': say 'tyrannically'(*regie*) and cruelly', a type of hendiadys.
7. 'I impose a punishment': *poenas sumo (-ere, sumpsi, sumptum) de* + ablative
8. 'which he deserves': use *dignus* in agreement with *poenas*.
9. 'as it is': *nunc vero.*
10. 'disease which afflicts our country' = (simply) 'disease of our country'.
11. 'for ever': *in perpetuum.*
12. 'I exile' = *in exsilium eicio, -ere, eieci, eiectum.*

4. Explorations

4. Explorations

1. From Virgil, *Aeneid* 1.1-38, 50-123, 157-79, 223-360, 387-92, 418-38 (A2 from June 2010 to June 2012)

Aeneid 1.272-96

hic iam ter centum totos regnabitur annos
gente sub Hectorea, donec regina sacerdos
Marte gravis geminam partu dabit Ilia prolem.
inde lupae fulvo nutricis tegmine laetus   275
Romulus excipiet gentem, et Mavortia condet
moenia Romanosque suo de nomine dicet.
his ego nec metas rerum nec tempora pono:
imperium sine fine dedi. quin aspera Iuno,
quae mare nunc terrasque metu caelumque fatigat,   280
consilia in melius referet, mecumque fovebit
Romanos, rerum dominos gentemque togatam:
sic placitum. veniet lustris labentibus aetas
cum domus Assaraci Pthiam clarasque Mycenas
servitio premet ac victis dominabitur Argis.   285
nascetur pulchra Troianus origine Caesar,
imperium Oceano, famam qui terminet astris,
Iulius, a magno demissum nomen Iulo.
hunc tu olim caelo spoliis Orientis onustum
accipies secura; vocabitur hic quoque votis.   290
aspera tum positis mitescent saecula bellis:
cana Fides et Vesta, Remo cum fratre Quirinus
iura dabunt; dirae ferro et compagibus artis
claudentur Belli portae; Furor impius intus
saeva sedens super arma et centum vinctus aenis   295
post tergum nodis fremet horridus ore cruento.

In the following commentary, which is intended to make clear the fact that there is no single way into these passages, we outline three different approaches. In fact these complement one another, and all of them no doubt contribute to the understanding of the excerpt. After you have read them, you may wish to ponder on which you consider to have been the most helpful approach for you. And can you think of any other approach?

1

One way of tackling this passage would be to consider the information given and the facts associated with it. In order to contextualise it, you would recall Aeneas in the storm wishing that he had been killed at Troy and then summoning up the resolution to encourage his colleagues, and move on to his mother Venus complaining to Jupiter about the treatment meted out to the pious man (253). These lines conclude Jupiter's great – and greatly affirmative – speech of reassurance. Now you can consider the passage itself.

hic: i.e. Alba Longa: see if you can find a photo of the Alban Lake. You may be interested to know that the Pope's summer residence at Castel Gandolfo is on the site. Kingship will continue for three whole centuries, fitting neatly into the scheme of three years of rule for Aeneas and thirty for Ascanius. Virgil alters the traditional four hundred years to fit this number scheme.

Hectorea: the mention of the Trojan champion reminds us that, though Troy is no more, the Trojan line will continue.

Marte: as Jupiter addresses Aeneas' mother, the goddess of love, we are told that the god of war will be an ancestor of the Romans. This is clearly important in view of the military nature of the Roman mission and it looks back to the first word of the poem, *arma*.

Ilia: otherwise known as Rhea Silvia, she is called by this name here, presumably to emphasise the connection with Troy (Ilium).

lupae: find a picture of an appropriate Roman coin or of the Capitoline wolf to confirm the centrality of this episode to the Roman self-image: cf. Livy 1.4.6-7 and *Aeneid* 8.631. Why was it so important to them? Does 275 mean that Romulus rejoiced in the covering of the she-wolf as she suckled him, or that he wore her hide after her death (cf. Propertius 4.10.20)?

moenia: the walls theme could be considered: cf. l.7 of the book. This links with the theme of foundation (*condet*): cf. 1.5 and 33.

nomine: consider the significance of the name Romulus (founder of Rome): note the long *o*: the English pronunciation is misleading.

Iuno: Juno's role in the poem could be considered. The deal she does with Jupiter in Book 12 could prove of particular interest.

rerum dominos gentemque togatam: 'warriors first, and then men of peace, the toga being the garment of civilian wear' (R.D. Williams). Is Williams right to highlight warfare as the Roman priority? The toga as an emblem of Roman identity calls for consideration.

283-5: the details of Rome's conquest of Greece, which became a Roman province in the second century BC, could be investigated. The mention of Phthia, Achilles' homeland, brings home the point that the defeat of Greece will counterbalance the fall of Troy.

Caesar: consideration of whether this is Julius Caesar or Augustus could prove stimulating. It would also lead you to valuable information about their conquests and achievements.

imperium: the actual extent of Rome's territory in the second half of the first century BC could be investigated.

Iulo: the association of Julius Caesar or Augustus (or both) with Iulus (Ascanius) in this line reminds us of the family's alleged descent from Venus. Have a look at a picture of the Prima Porta statue of Augustus, with Cupid (Iulus' half-brother) at his leg. Also refer back to 286.

289-90: *spoliis Orientis* would seem to be a reference to the defeats of Antony and Cleopatra at the Battle of Actium and later at Alexandria; so we may well be talking about Augustus, who will one day be deified (like Aeneas – *quoque*). But Julius Caesar was deified too.

291-3: find out more about the *pax Augusta*, Fides and Vesta (see Austin's or Williams' notes) and the Gates of War in the temple of Janus, closed in 29 BC and 25 BC under Augustus.

Furor: Jupiter here responds to Venus' complaint that the man of *pietas* is being so ill rewarded (253). Servius wrote that the picture of *Furor impius* was based on a painting by Apelles (Pliny, *Natural History* 35.93) which Augustus placed in his own forum.

2

A second approach could take into account the literary qualities of the passage. Inevitably we take our own line – which may change at any moment – about a number of features, and you may well disagree with much or indeed with everything that we have written. Talking about such disagreements can be a particularly valuable activity. One obvious comment on which we may all feel able to concur is that the momentous lines in this excerpt about the greatness of Rome are made resonant in part by frequent use of *m*s and *n*s.

The first line has no poetic colouring and relies for its emphatic tread on the way that meaning is reinforced by the proliferation of spondees and the impersonal passive. The absence of end-stopping in 272 and 273 leads us forward with the sweep of inevitability to the birth of Romulus. The mention of the dead Hector injects a stab of pathos but this is counterbalanced by Romulus' joy (*laetus*) and the intimacy of the suckling wolf (*nutricis*) and then overwhelmed by the thematic reference to the walls of Rome and the boundless Roman empire: *m*s and *n*s reverberate. The adjective *aspera* reminds us of Juno's terrifying role in the poem, but even she will alter her thinking and cherish the Romans, who are summed up in the nobly resonant line 282.

The crisp *sic placitum* makes it clear that, according to Jupiter, there will be no problems. As the years slip by, the descendants of the Trojans (Assaracus was Aeneas' great-grandfather) will enslave and lord it over Greece (*dominabitur*: cf. *dominos*, 282): the unusual and therefore striking monosyllable before the caesura in 285 adds a note of metrical violence to the suppression of the former enemy.

The noble and stately lines that follow are humanised by the use of *pulchra* to describe Caesar's origins (whether he is Julius Caesar or Augustus) – presumably referring to Venus, the mother of Aeneas, intellectualised by the aetiology[1] of the name Julius (with *Iulius* and *Iulo* set in balance at either end of 288; cf. 267-8), and given ballast by the reference to Eastern conquests. And the deification of Caesar is described obliquely (Venus will receive him in heaven; he will be invoked in prayers), thus avoiding eulogistic excess.

The famous lines that conclude the excerpt vividly and memorably convey the inauguration of peace. Just as *aspera Iuno* will become beneficent to the Romans, so will the *aspera saecula* become gentle with the cessation of warfare. The ultra-Roman deities Fides and Vesta will ensure justice; Romulus (Quirinus) will be in harmony with the brother he killed (292-3): the gates of War will be closed – effortfully because of the *ferro et compagibus artis*, as is conveyed in the clash between ictus (metrical beat) and speech stress in the otherwise assertively simple *claudentur Belli portae*. The passage concludes with the extraordinary portrait of *Furor impius* chained and behind the doors: the details will, of course, well repay consideration. The words *furor* and *impius*, as you will know well by now, re-echo throughout the poem and here Jupiter tells Venus that the qualities they represent will be stifled. But the hissing *ss* of 294-5 and the clash between ictus and speech stress before the last three words of the final line ally with the meaning to fight against Jupiter's supremely confident reassurance.

3

A third approach would contextualise the passage within Book 1 and the *Aeneid* as a whole.

Like Thetis and Athena complaining to Zeus about the maltreatment of Achilles and Odysseus respectively (at *Iliad* 1.495-510 and *Odyssey* 5.5-20), Venus protests to Jupiter that the promise of Aeneas' destiny is not being fulfilled. In one of the poem's greatest patriotic passages (from which this is an excerpt), Jupiter, smiling and 'with the expression with which he makes the heavens and the changing skies turn sunny' (Williams), kisses her and reassures her. She should lay aside her fear. The destiny of Rome will be fulfilled.

While Jupiter does acknowledge that a long war will have to be fought with the Italians (263-6), his soaring rhetoric fails to respond to the vast weight of suffering involved in the Roman future. The smooth progression of Rome's mission as the years slip by (283) takes little account of its tragic consequences, unlike the pageant of heroes in Book 6 where, for example, the grim dilemma of Brutus and the tragic death of Marcellus are given telling

---

[1] The study of causes and origins.

98

emphasis. Juno's role in the poem is acknowledged (280), but its focus is on her transformation into a beneficent force. The tone is very different from that of the poet's anguished address to the Muse about her malevolence at lines 8-11.

The resonant lines about the greatness of the Roman empire – with the superb hyperbole of 287 – culminate in an evocation of a golden age under Augustus – or Julius Caesar – when wars will cease. There is no ironising of the splendours of these lines: again the pageant of heroes may be a helpful point of reference, since it ends in a very different way with Anchises bursting into tears and Aeneas and the Sibyl leaving the underworld by the gate of false dreams: thus optimism is emphatically subverted. In our passage Augustus – or Caesar – is to be deified. Romulus and Remus are to give laws: their fraternal strife, Rome's original sin (cf. Horace, *Epode* 7.17-20), is totally omitted. Most strikingly, the climactic assurance that Furor will be shackled in the Augustan golden age is magnificent, but also magnificently oblivious to the role that Furor will play in the poem. The *Aeneid*, of course, concludes with its pious hero possessed by this emotion and the epic as a whole tugs against Jupiter's confident assertion here. It may be significant that we are told nothing about Venus's reaction.

Yet Jupiter's words are true as far as they go and the resplendent rhetoric of his speech, placed so early in the poem, is important in assuring the reader that Rome's future greatness will have a civilising grandeur that validates it. The fact that elsewhere the suffering involved and the fate of the victims are given such poignant emphasis will cause us to recall Jupiter's words with a complex of emotions, but their noble optimism makes them profoundly telling in communicating why Aeneas has to endure. However fraught with suffering, the Roman mission is as inspirational as it is great.

2. Catullus 1, 2, 3, 4, 7-13, 22, 63, 70 (A2 June 2010 to June 2012); 2, 3, 5, 7, 8, 11, 51, 58, 64 (73-250), 68, 76, 79, 83, 85, 86, 87, 92 (Pre-U from 2010 to 2012)

(a) Catullus 3

lugete, o Veneres Cupidinesque,
et quantum est hominum venustiorum:
passer mortuus est meae puellae,
passer, deliciae meae puellae,
quem plus illa oculis suis amabat –   5
nam mellitus erat suamque norat
ipsam tam bene quam puella matrem,
nec sese a gremio illius movebat,
sed circumsiliens modo huc modo illuc
ad solam dominam usque pipiabat: 10

qui nunc it per iter tenebricosum
illud, unde negant redire quemquam.
at uobis male sit, malae tenebrae
Orci, quae omnia bella devoratis:
tam bellum mihi passerem abstulistis. 15
o factum male! o miselle passer!
tua nunc opera meae puellae
flendo turgiduli rubent ocelli.

The Greek Anthology (a vast collection of short Greek poems) includes a number of poems about the death of animals, but none of them approaches Catullus in his control of tone in this lament. Emotion flows naturally in his poem while it shifts its register through its various stages: 1-5: a statement of the cause of mourning; 6-10: a summary of the qualities and attainments of the dead sparrow; 11-12: who is now hopping along on his final journey; 13-16: an outraged outburst against death; 17-18: a final vignette of the mourning girl.

The use of the animated hendecasyllable metre undermines excessive seriousness, as does *Veneres Cupidinesque* (line 1; cf.13.12) which sets us in the world of Hellenistic *putti*. *Veneres* leads us straight to a favourite word of Catullus and his set, *venustus* – *bellus* in 14 and 15 is another, and the same world is conjured up by the affectionate diminutives of 15 and 16. There is a constant tug in the poem between the deeply serious concept of mourning and the colloquialism of the language (*venustus* (2), *mellitus* (6), *modo huc modo illuc* (9), *male* (13 and 16), *bellus* (14 and 15)). The simple diction is particularly effective in the hopping alliteration of 11 (*qui nunc it per iter*) which is followed by the resonant line about the finality of death. The sparrow, the most diminutive of birds, has become part of a drama which is too grand for it, just as the curse on Orcus, the king of the underworld, (13-14) is out of all proportion to what has actually happened.

You may wish to trace what we are told about the girlfriend's relationship with her pet sparrow, starting with the strikingly straightforward statement of lines 3-5. What is the effect of the repetition of *passer* in these lines? And of *pipiabat* in line10? What do the last two lines suggest as the true cause of the poet's distress?

(b) Catullus 7

quaeris, quot mihi basiationes
tuae, Lesbia, sint satis superque?
quam magnus numerus Libyssae harenae
lasarpiciferis iacet Cyrenis
oraclum Iovis inter aestuosi 5
et Batti veteris sacrum sepulcrum;
aut quam sidera multa, cum tacet nox,

furtivos hominum vident amores:
tam te basia multa basiare
vesano satis et super Catullo est,   10
quae nec pernumerare curiosi
possint nec mala fascinare lingua.

There is likely to be profitable disagreement about this poem. It makes a clear pairing with poem 5, the celebratory *vivamus, mea Lesbia, atque amemus*, in which Catullus invites his girl to add kiss to kiss beyond the capacity of mathematics. In that poem there is an outside world of judgemental old men (2-3) and malevolent observers (12-13), but the lovers will be beyond their reach.

How celebratory is poem 7? It is here that opinions are likely to differ. An affirmative reading may find confirmation in the last two lines, which echo the early poem in seeking innumerable kisses so that the *curiosi* cannot count their number and put a jinx on the lovers. However, it may be possible to find a note of hectic desperation in the poem. Suspicion may be awakened in line 1 with the use of the portentous word *basiationes* for 'kisses' (as opposed to the simple *basia*): one of the translators renders this 'kissifications'. To wish for as many kisses as there are sands in the desert or stars in the night sky is unimpeachably romantic; but to invoke the silphium-bearing nature of Cyrene[2] and the torrid heat of the desert may add a disconcerting note of sickness and sun-stroke to the poem: the juice of the silphium plant (asafoetida) was a cure against bites, boils, gout, dropsy, asthma, epilepsy and pleurisy (see Godwin's excellent note); and Catullus later tells us that he is mad (*vesano*, 10). Then the stars are portrayed as the witnesses not of life-enhancing but of stolen love.

The lively hendecasyllable metre does not help us in the matter of which line the poet wishes us to take. It could be celebratory or hectically posing. It will be clear that we view Catullus 7 as a neurotic outpouring, but you may think differently. We can surely agree that this is a powerful and evocative poem.

3. Tacitus, *Annals* 14.1-16 (A2 June 2010 to June 2012)

Annals 14.1-2

[1] Gaio Vipstano C. Fonteio consulibus diu meditatum scelus non ultra Nero distulit, vetustate imperii coalita audacia et flagrantior in dies amore Poppaeae, quae sibi matrimonium et discidium Octaviae incolumi Agrippina haud sperans crebris criminationibus, aliquando per facetias incusare principem et pupillum vocare, qui iussis alienis obnoxius non modo imperii, sed libertatis

---

[2] You will wish to investigate the literary overtones of the Cyrene location and the mention of Battus. There are clear references to the Hellenistic poet Callimachus here. Does such self-conscious poeticising work against an impression of 'the spontaneous overflow of powerful feeling' (Wordsworth)?

etiam indigeret. cur enim differri nuptias suas? formam scilicet displicere et triumphales avos, an fecunditatem et verum animum? timeri ne uxor saltem iniurias patrum, iram populi adversus superbiam avaritiamque matris aperiat. quod si nurum Agrippina non nisi filio infestam ferre posset, redderetur ipsa Othonis coniugio: ituram quoquo terrarum, ubi audiret potius contumelias imperatoris quam viseret periculis eius immixta. haec atque talia lacrimis et arte adulterae penetrantia nemo prohibebat, cupientibus cunctis infringi potentiam matris et credente nullo usque ad caedem eius duratura filii odia.

[2] tradit Cluvius ardore retinendae Agrippinam potentiae eo usque provectam, ut medio diei, cum id temporis Nero per vinum et epulas incalesceret, offerret se saepius temulento comptam et incesto paratam; iamque lasciva oscula et praenuntias flagitii blanditias adnotantibus proximis, Senecam contra muliebres inlecebras subsidium a femina petivisse, immissamque Acten libertam, quae simul suo periculo et infamia Neronis anxia deferret pervulgatum esse incestum gloriante matre, nec toleraturos milites profani principis imperium.

The annalistic structure of the work – the events are unfolded a year at a time – means that each new year begins with the straightforward naming of the consuls in an ablative absolute. The objective tone here flings into arresting relief what comes next. Nero's long meditation is over. He postpones the crime (matricide, but Tacitus keeps us in suspense about this till the end of chapter 1) no longer.

One obvious way into this passage would be to examine the progress of the first sentence with its expressive shifts of tone. The subject (*Nero*) comes after the object (*scelus*): he is associated with criminality at this, his first appearance in the sentence (and of course the book). There is constant balancing of ideas. Nero's boldness has grown because of the length of his reign just as his passion for Poppaea has blazed more and more from day to day; she has set her hopes on marriage to Nero, which would inevitably involve his divorce from Octavia.[3] She attacks him but with accusations and mockery. He is both the emperor and a little schoolboy. He is deprived not only of his supreme authority but of his liberty too. (If you had been Nero, how would you have responded to Poppaea's onslaught?) We have been led without a break into Poppaea's hopes and then into the reproaches and taunts which she aims at Nero. You may well wish to investigate the historical validity of those hopes, reproaches and taunts. What does the ablative absolute *incolumi Agrippina* tell us is going on in her mind?

The scornfully ironic tone of the next sentence, rammed home by *scilicet*, will certainly repay examination. The rhetorical balancing of the two pairs of aspects in which she sarcastically suggests that she may be displeasing to Nero makes the scorn even more pointed. The passive infinitive *timeri* (was it being

---

[3] The divorce with Octavia would of course have to precede the marriage, but Tacitus puts the marriage first. This adjustment of the order of events is known as *hysteron proteron*: generally the more important event is placed first.

feared?) has a splendid unspecivity which heightens the fact that it is obviously aimed at Nero. She sets the sufferings of the senators and anger of the people against the pride and greed of Agrippina. The black humour of the allegation that Agrippina can only tolerate a daughter who hates her son leads to a calculated sexual barb: she would prefer to go back to her husband Otho and hear of Nero's humiliations than to witness them and share her dangers. Perhaps the main point of her playing the timorous woman is to communicate to Nero the suggestion that *he* is in danger.

We have followed the contours of Poppaea's thoughts since line 3, the opening sentence in effect continuing until line 11. How do you react to her in these lines? What is the effect of T.'s use of indirect rather than direct speech here? I have used the expression 'black humour' above. Do you feel that there *is* in fact humour in these words? What does Tacitus tell us about the way they were delivered – and received – immediately after he ceases to report them? What is the effect of the word *filio*, the penultimate word in the chapter?[4]

The overall tone of this passage has been established. In the long sentence we have included from chapter 2 which unfolds with an equal expressiveness to the first eleven lines of chapter 1, the following questions may be worth pursuing. How persuasive is Tacitus' distancing of himself from the allegations of incipient incest by the attribution of this account to Cluvius? (We are told later that most authors support his version.) What is given as Agrippina's motivation? How is Nero's decadence communicated? Is Acte's status as a freedwoman relevant? What is her motivation? What is she to persuade Nero that his mother is boasting of? What precisely is she to tell him that the soldiers will not tolerate? Do you feel that Tacitus is going too far in his hostile presentation of women in this passage? How, in the passage as a whole, is the idea of an observant court communicated?

4. Livy 23.2-9 (A2 from June 2010 to June 2012)

Livy 23.2

[2] inde Capuam flectit iter, luxuriantem longa felicitate atque indulgentia fortunae, maxime tamen inter corrupta omnia licentia plebis sine modo liber-tatem exercentis. senatum et sibi et plebi obnoxium Pacuvius Calavius fecerat, nobilis idem ac popularis homo, ceterum malis artibus nanctus opes. is cum eo forte anno, quo res male gesta ad Trasumennum est, in summo magistratu esset, iam diu infestam senatui plebem ratus per occasionem novandi res magnum ausuram facinus ut, si in ea loca Hannibal cum victore exercitu venisset, trucidato senatu traderet Capuam Poenis, improbus homo sed non ad extremum perditus, cum mallet incolumi quam eversa re publica dominari, nullam autem incolumem esse orbatam publico consilio crederet, rationem iniit qua et senatum servaret et obnoxium sibi ac plebi faceret. vocato senatu

---

[4] Note how *potentiam matris* and *filii odia* are balanced in a chiasmus.

cum sibi defectionis ab Romanis consilium placiturum nullo modo, nisi necessarium fuisset, praefatus esset, quippe qui liberos ex Ap. Claudi filia haberet filiamque Romam nuptum M. Livio dedisset; ceterum maiorem multo rem magisque timendam instare; non enim per defectionem ad tollendum ex civitate senatum plebem spectare sed per caedem senatus vacuam rem publicam tradere Hannibali ac Poenis velle; eo se periculo posse liberare eos si permittant sibi et certaminum in re publica obliti credant, – cum omnes victi metu permitterent, 'claudam' inquit 'in curia vos et, tamquam et ipse cogitati facinoris particeps, approbando consilia quibus nequiquam adversarer viam saluti vestrae inueniam. in hoc fidem, quam voltis ipsi, accipite.' fide data egressus claudi curiam iubet praesidiumque in vestibulo relinquit ne quis adire curiam iniussu suo neve inde egredi possit.

Some contextualisation is necessary here. You should investigate the devastating victories of Hannibal over the Romans at Trasimene and Cannae and think about the likely reactions of the Italian cities which the triumphant Carthaginian armies approached. This is now the situation that threatens Capua as Hannibal veers (*flectit*) towards it.

In what follows we shoot a volley of questions at you. These are intended to help you to elicit the full meaning of each sentence without telling you what to think!

How is Capua described in the first sentence? (The hedonism and depravity of the city are referred to again in 4.4-5.) What seems to be Livy's attitude to the freedom of the common people? What do we discover in the next sentence to be their attitude to the senate?

We are now introduced to Pacuvius Calavius. (He does not reappear after this episode and the amount of detail allocated to him draws attention to itself. As J.C. Yardley suggests, 'the entire Pacuvius story may be a highly worked-up account, focusing exaggeratedly on only one out of several leaders'.) Over whom has he gained influence, and how? What does he think that the people will do if Hannibal arrives? What does Livy appear to feel about this? (It may be helpful to look up *trucido* in the Oxford Latin Dictionary: you need to use a dictionary which gives examples of the usage of the word by Latin authors to get a rounded sense of its meaning.) What do you feel is Livy's view of Pacuvius? Why does he judge him *non ad extremum perditus*? What is Pacuvius' plan? Is there any point in Livy's repetition of the idea of the senate's dependence on Pacuvius and the people? In the sentence beginning *vocato senatu*, how does Pacuvius support his claim that he would not support defection from Rome unless it was necessary? How does he then go on to frighten the senate? The indirect statement concludes at *credant*. What is the effect of the change to direct speech at *claudam*? How does the final sentence show Pacuvius as a puppet master?

Do you believe this story? If you had been a senator, would you have trusted

Pacuvius? If Livy has here simplified or invented history, what do you imagine was his aim?

5. Virgil, *Aeneid* 4.1-299 (A2 from June 2013 to June 2015)

Aeneid 4.66-89

est mollis flamma medullas
interea et tacitum vivit sub pectore vulnus.
uritur infelix Dido totaque vagatur
urbe furens, qualis coniecta cerva sagitta,
quam procul incautam nemora inter Cresia fixit   70
pastor agens telis liquitque volatile ferrum
nescius: illa fuga silvas saltusque peragrat
Dictaeos; haeret lateri letalis harundo.
nunc media Aenean secum per moenia ducit
Sidoniasque ostentat opes urbemque paratam,   75
incipit effari mediaque in voce resistit;
nunc eadem labente die convivia quaerit,
Iliacosque iterum demens audire labores
exposcit pendetque iterum narrantis ab ore.
post ubi digressi, lumenque obscura vicissim   80
luna premit suadentque cadentia sidera somnos,
sola domo maeret vacua stratisque relictis
incubat. illum absens absentem auditque videtque,
aut gremio Ascanium genitoris imagine capta
detinet, infandum si fallere possit amorem.   85
non coeptae adsurgunt turres, non arma iuuentus
exercet portusve aut propugnacula bello
tuta parant: pendent opera interrupta minaeque
murorum ingentes aequataque machina caelo.

Despite the prophets and the rituals which Dido performs, the flame and the wound of love – think of Cupid's torch and his bow and arrows – do their work deep inside her. The metaphorical symbols of love will become literal at the end of the book on what will be her funeral pyre. The harsh monosyllable *est* ('eats' – the *e* is long) is strikingly placed at the head of the sentence. Is it the flame or the marrow of her bones that is *mollis* (the adjective could go either with *flamma* or *medullas*)? Either way, the alliteration of *m*s and *l*s conveys the gentle process through which the fire does its devastating work. What does *tacitum … vulnus* mean? Is the wound silent because Dido does not realise what is happening to her, or because she does not confess her love to Aeneas, its object?[5]

Infelix Dido – the poet's sympathetic expression occurs three times in the

---

[5] Keith Maclennan interestingly points out to us that the wound hisses (*stridit vulnus*) at l.689.

book (68, 450, 596, cf. 529) – is on fire with love, and the *furor* which now possesses her finds expression in aimless motion. The famous simile of the deer wounded by a shepherd calls for detailed analysis. The obvious correspondences with the situation of Dido (the deer) and Aeneas (the shepherd) should not distract us from its fundamental pathos and its evocation of pain,[6] and with its location in the forested uplands of Crete we are far distant from the ordered coastal city that Dido has been building. The shepherd is unaware that he has hit the deer. What does this tell us about Aeneas? The *sagitta* is the arrow of love which cannot be pulled out (*haeret*).

Lines 74-5 remind us of the public Dido – the dynamic leader whom Venus has described in Book 1 (360-8) – and renews the poem's theme of the walled city, but 76 portrays her as stumbling as she speaks, and 77-9 show her trapped in an obsessive cycle of repetition as she repeats the banquet in Book 1 and madly demands that Aeneas tell his story once more (Books 2 and 3 will thus be constantly repeated) and hangs from his lips as he does so.

They part and the late hour urges sleep. Line 81 should be scanned and its sound savoured. The last three words form a wonderfully soothing cadence with the verse stress coinciding with the speech stress. But in contrast Dido can find no rest. How is her obsession with Aeneas conveyed in lines 82-5? What is the effect caused by *absens absentem*? Why is the love *infandum*?

In lines 86-9 we discover that all work on the city and all military training have stopped. The crane simply standing there idle is an evocative symbol of halted activity. Dido's private passion has taken her over: it has eclipsed her public persona as queen of Carthage. What do you feel about this? In modern literature, love is often portrayed as life-enhancing. Why is Dido's love for Aeneas such a tragedy for her?

6. Propertius 3.8, 10, 12, 13, 15, 16, 21, 25 (A2 June 2013 to June 2015)

Propertius 3.10

> mirabar, quidnam visissent mane Camenae,
>   ante meum stantes sole rubente torum.
> natalis nostrae signum misere puellae
>   et manibus faustos ter crepuere sonos.
> transeat hic sine nube dies, stent aere venti,   5
>   ponat et in sicco molliter unda minax.
> aspiciam nullos hodierna luce dolentis,
>   et Niobae lacrimas supprimat ipse lapis;

---

[6] This is memorably recapitulated by Matthew Arnold in *Sohrab and Rustum*, 503-6:
>   most like the roar
> Of some pain'd desert-lion, who all day
> Hath trail'd the hunter's javelin in his side,
> And comes at night to die upon the sand.

alcyonum positis requiescant ora querelis;
    increpet absumptum nec sua mater Ityn.   10
tuque, o cara mihi, felicibus edita pennis,
    surge et poscentis iusta precare deos.
at primum pura somnum tibi discute lympha,
    et nitidas presso pollice finge comas;
dein qua primum oculos cepisti veste Properti   15
    indue, nec vacuum flore relinque caput;
et pete, qua polles, ut sit tibi forma perennis,
    inque meum semper stent tua regna caput.
inde coronatas ubi ture piaveris aras,
    luxerit et tota flamma secunda domo,   20
sit mensae ratio, noxque inter pocula currat,
    et crocino nares murreus ungat onyx.

The poet wakes up to find the Camenae (the Muses) standing in front of his bed against the background of an appropriately poetic (Homeric) rosy-fingered dawn. His muzzy state is reflected in the heavily spondaic opening line with its alliteration of drowsy *m*s and *n*s. The Muses are a sign that it is his girlfriend's birthday – presumably they are expecting him to write a birthday poem – and with favourable augury they clap their hands three times. Line 4 has a splendid crispness: the poet is now fully awake.

He then expresses his wish for a day of perfect calm: may the sky be cloudless; may no winds blow; may the sea be stilled. When he goes on to hope that he will see no one sorrowing on this day, we may feel that he is wanting something unattainable – but then why not? That is what wishes often are.

Propertius' use of mythology in the following lines calls for investigation: what exactly are the stories referred to here? You will find that they all contain tragic elements. The poet distances the tears of Niobe, the complaints of the halcyons and the laments of Itys' mother Procne, but you may feel that he is evoking a world of sorrow that can perhaps be banished for a halcyon day but still underlies the human experience. Indeed, it may be precisely because of the inevitability of tragedy that it is vital to seize opportunities for happiness with both hands. (Is it possible to generalise about Propertius' use of mythology?)

The bird imagery of line 10 continues with the happy auguries with which the poet tells Cynthia to get out of bed and to say her prayers. He visualises her performing her toilette, imagining this with lively evocativeness: the freshness of the water which shakes off somnolence; the tactile detail of her coiffeur; the arresting recollection in Propertius' request that she put on the dress she was wearing when she first caught his eye.

She is to pray that her beauty will last for ever and thus ensure her power over Propertius; he *wants* to be under her sway. Of course her beauty will not last for ever. Indeed, Propertius visualises his Cynthia as an unwanted old woman in 3.25.11-12, 15-18. You will have to decide whether the unreality of the wish undermines the poem, or adds fuel to the heady 'Gather ye rosebuds while ye may' atmosphere of the last two lines of the excerpt and the rest of the poem. These lines are preceded by mention of another religious ritual, to be performed with brilliant illumination (lines 19-20). And then the poet's thoughts turn away from religion and rush forward to the night. The *mensae ratio* will be replaced by hectic drinking and the scent of perfume: the sense of smell is luxuriously invoked in line 22 where not only is the expression *naris ungat* arresting in itself, but, as Camps remarks, 'every word is colourful (and resonant)'.

Some have found a worrying undercurrent in this poem. The unreal nature of the poet's wishes and the rampant hedonism which develops from lines 21-2 may suggest that serious anxiety underlies his excessive optimism. On the other hand, what do *you* wish for on your girlfriend's or boyfriend's birthday? How realistic are your wishes? And do you want to have an impossibly good time with them? Does this mean that you are anxious? You will have to make up your own mind about this.

7. Tacitus, *Annals* 15.20-23, 33-45 (A2 from June 2013 to June 2015)

Annals 15.44

[44] mox petita dis piacula aditique Sibyllae libri, ex quibus supplicatum Volcano et Cereri Proserpinaeque ac propitiata Iuno per matronas, primum in Capitolio, deinde apud proximum mare, unde hausta aqua templum et simulacrum deae perspersum est; et sellisternia ac pervigilia celebravere feminae, quibus mariti erant.

sed non ope humana, non largitionibus principis aut deum placamentis decedebat infamia quin iussum incendium crederetur. ergo abolendo rumori Nero subdidit reos et quaesitissimis poenis adfecit quos per flagitia invisos vulgus Christianos appellabat. auctor nominis eius Christus Tiberio imperitante per procuratorem Pontium Pilatum supplicio adfectus erat; repressaque in praesens exitiablilis superstitio rursum erumpebat, non modo per Iudaeam, originem eius mali, sed per urbem etiam quo cuncta undique atrocia aut pudenda confluunt celebranturque. igitur primum correpti qui fatebantur, deinde indicio eorum multitudo ingens haud proinde in crimine incendii quam odio humani generis convicti sunt. et pereuntibus addita ludibria, ut ferarum tergis contecti laniatu canum interirent, aut crucibus adfixi aut flammandi, atque ubi defecisset dies in usum nocturni luminis urerentur. hortos suos ei spectaculo Nero obtulerat et circense ludicrum edebat, habitu aurigae permixtus plebi vel curriculo insistens. unde quamquam adversus sontes et novissima exempla meritos miseratio oriebatur, tamquam non utilitate publica, sed in saevitiam unius absumerentur.

The historian has just dealt with the practical measures taken against future outbreaks of fire. He now turns to the attempts to appease the gods. The passage about the Christians is thus preceded by an exposition of traditional Roman religious practices. Consult the notes of your edition for the Sibylline books, the particular gods consulted, the role of the women, and the religious significance of water. Why do you think Tacitus has gone into this amount of detail?

Near the start of the next section there is a reference to Nero's generosity, but in Tacitus a favourable reference to the emperor is not likely to stay unclouded for long. Who do you imagine he wants us to believe started the fire? Why do you think that Tacitus does not simply tell us this? In the sentence beginning with *ergo*, what is the effect of the words *subdidit* and *quaesitissimos*?

With this historian, and in view of the fact that Nero is scapegoating the Christians, we might have expected that they would receive favourable treatment, but this is far from being the case. It may be a useful exercise to make a list of all the words and phrases in the rest of this passage (from *quos per flagitia*) which Tacitus uses to blacken them. Do you feel that the detailed exposition of Roman religious practices with which the passage began was intended to throw into relief the *exitiabilis superstitio* of Christianity – or is Tacitus simply recording the events at they happened? (What was your response to the question at the end of our first paragraph?) What point is being made about Rome in the relative clause after *per urbem etiam*? What do you imagine that the Christians confessed to? This could be an apt point to consider why Christianity presented the Romans, who were normally extremely tolerant of religions other than their own, with particular problems.

Examine the ways in which the executions of Christians were rendered farcical (*ludibria*). Why is it particularly appropriate that some of them should be crucified? What does all this tell us about Roman ideas of entertainment? Why do the people start to feel pity for men they regarded as guilty and deserving of extraordinary punishment (*sontes et novissima exempla meritos*)? What points are being made about Nero when he is portrayed as *habitu aurigae permixtus plebi vel curriculo insistens*? Do you think that Tacitus gets away with presenting the Christians *both* as detested criminals *and* objects of sympathy? What point is he making by showing them as the latter?

8. Sallust, *Bellum Catilinae*, 14-29 (A2 from June 2013 to June 2015), 5-39 (Pre-U from 2010 to 2012)

Bellum Catilinae 24-5

[24] igitur comitiis habitis consules declarantur M. Tullius et C. Antonius. quod factum primo popularis coniurationis concusserat. neque tamen Catilinae furor minuebatur, sed in dies plura agitare: arma per Italiam locis oppor-

tunis parare, pecuniam sua aut amicorum fide sumptam mutuam Faesulas ad Manlium quendam portare, qui postea princeps fuit belli faciundi. ea tempestate plurimos cuiusque generis homines adscivisse sibi dicitur, mulieres etiam aliquot, quae primo ingentis sumptus stupro corporis toleraverant, post ubi aetas tantum modo quaestui neque luxuriae modum fecerat, aes alienum grande conflaverant. per eas se Catilina credebat posse servitia urbana sollicitare, urbem incendere, viros earum vel adiungere sibi vel interficere.

[25] sed in iis erat Sempronia, quae multa saepe virilis audaciae facinora conmiserat. haec mulier genere atque forma, praeterea viro, liberis satis fortunata fuit; litteris Graecis et Latinis docta, psallere et saltare elegantius quam necesse est probae, multa alia, quae instrumenta luxuriae sunt. sed ei cariora semper omnia quam decus atque pudicitia fuit; pecuniae an famae minus parceret, haud facile discerneres; lubido sic accensa, ut saepius peteret viros quam peteretur. sed ea saepe antehac fidem prodiderat, creditum abiuraverat, caedis conscia fuerat; luxuria atque inopia praeceps abierat. verum ingenium eius haud absurdum: posse versus facere, iocum movere, sermone uti vel modesto vel molli vel procaci; prorsus multae facetiae multusque lepos inerat.

The opening sentence conveys the situation in unadorned, factual language. *comitiis habitis* and *consules declarantur* – note the vivid historic present – are the technical expressions for conducting an election and the presiding magistrate's declaration of the winners. Cicero and Antonius have been elected consul. When Cicero defeated Catiline before, we are now told, this had led to the first convulsion of popular conspiracy. Cicero's election does not lead to any lessening of Catiline's frenzy: you will wish here to consider the force of the word *furor*, the opposite quality to *pietas* in Virgil's *Aeneid*. The imperfect *minuebatur* finds expression in frenzied action and that is linked with financial rashness (*pecuniam ... mutuam*). Here we are introduced to Manlius who will be the first to launch the fighting (on 27 October 63 BC). His previous anonymity is conveyed by the perhaps contemptuous use of *quendam* and omission of his *praenomen* (Gaius). Among the large numbers whom Catiline will call to his side are several wives whose financial acquisitiveness (and irresponsibility) and lack of morality are rammed home. Is there something cruel about the biographer's statement that the passage of time had restricted their ability to raise money through their bodies, but not set a limit on their abandoned life style (*luxuriae*)? Through them (presumably by means of the money they brought with them), Catiline believed he would rouse the slaves of the city, and set it on fire. (Fire is a frequent concomitant of *furor* in the *Aeneid*.) He hoped to recruit their husbands or to kill them: *interficere* is placed with devastating emphasis at the end of the sentence, its climactic status stressed by the fact that the last element in the tricolon (*viros ... interficere*) follows the others in asyndeton. According to Appian (*Bella Civilia* 2.2), Catiline was backed by many women who hoped that they could kill their husbands as a result of the uprising. The challenge to Roman, indeed to human values, comes across strongly here.

The scornful portrayal of the women who joined Catiline leads naturally to the portrayal of Sempronia. There is no further reference to her in the monograph apart from the fact that the conference with the Allobroges took place at her house (40.5) – so why has Sallust included her? It is worthwhile to compare her portrait here with the sketch of Catiline (5.1-8; cf. 15) and, as one of the editors (J.T. Ramsey) remarks, 'she is, in a sense, his female counterpart: both were descended from noble families, talented, daring and depraved'. Sempronia's inclusion may reflect the notoriously un-Roman fact that women were involved in what would become public action. She may also be emblematic of the perversion and misuse of admirable talents – as well as the attraction of those talents. You may find it valuable to make lists of her good and bad qualities. The Latin of the portrayal is supremely balanced and well-ordered. Does it prove an effective medium through which to convey her multifarious qualities with their mixture of the base and the estimable? What do you take Sallust to mean by *psallere et saltare elegantius quam necesse est probae*? Does this portrayal come to life for you? Can you believe in it? What evidence of her high culture do you find in the portrait? Do you feel that Sallust is being excessively judgemental and puritanical? Do you admire Sempronia? Does Sallust? Why do you think that Sallust concludes with a generally favourable list of qualities, ending with *multus lepos*? How far do you feel that these chapters are coloured by Cicero's propaganda against Catiline?

9. Virgil, *Aeneid* 8.1-519 (Pre-U for 2010 to 2012)

Aeneid 8.193-224

hic spelunca fuit vasto summota recessu,	
semihominis Caci facies quam dira tenebat	
solis inaccessam radiis; semperque recenti	195
caede tepebat humus, foribusque adfixa superbis	
ora virum tristi pendebant pallida tabo.	
huic monstro Volcanus erat pater: illius atros	
ore vomens ignes magna se mole ferebat.	
attulit et nobis aliquando optantibus aetas	200
auxilium adventumque dei. nam maximus ultor	
tergemini nece Geryonae spoliisque superbus	
Alcides aderat taurosque hac victor agebat	
ingentis, vallemque boves amnemque tenebant.	
at furis Caci mens effera, ne quid inausum	205
aut intractatum scelerisve dolive fuisset,	
quattuor a stabulis praestanti corpore tauros	

auertit, totidem forma superante iuvencas.
atque hos, ne qua forent pedibus vestigia rectis,
cauda in speluncam tractos versisque viarum   210
indiciis raptor saxo occultabat opaco;
quaerenti nulla ad speluncam signa ferebant.
interea, cum iam stabulis saturata moveret
Amphitryoniades armenta abitumque pararet,
discessu mugire boves atque omne querelis   215
impleri nemus et colles clamore relinqui.
reddidit una boum vocem vastoque sub antro
mugiit et Caci spem custodita fefellit.
hic vero Alcidae furiis exarserat atro
felle dolor: rapit arma manu nodisque grauatum   220
robur, et aerii cursu petit ardua montis.
tum primum nostri Cacum videre timentem
turbatumque oculi; fugit ilicet ocior Euro
speluncamque petit, pedibus timor addidit alas.

The tale of how Hercules killed the monster Cacus (note that the *a* is long) and so saved the early inhabitants of the site of Rome is one of primitive violence. (How does this violence fit in with the themes of the poem as a whole?) Evander has pointed out to Aeneas, in lines 190-3 (note the dissonant sibilants), the rocky landscape around the location of Cacus' former cave. You may wish to look ahead to the primitively totemic pinnacle of flint, the nesting place of the carrion birds who feasted on the monster's victims (233-5) which was torn down by Hercules and caused this jagged expanse.

In lines 193-4 the giant is introduced to us in a strikingly abstract periphrasis (the terrible appearance of the half-man Cacus) as a creature of the darkness inhabiting a vast cave beneath the rock, a deep recess which the sun's rays never reach. Horrific details are now added: the ground always warm with fresh slaughter and the putrefying human heads hanging as grisly trophies from the doors. The fire-god Vulcan was Cacus' father and it was his black fires that the giant belched forth. You may wish to consider the part that fire plays in the poem: it is usually destructive but it can have the radiance of a halo: see e.g. 2.682-4 (Iulus) and 8.678-81 (Augustus). Cacus' black fires fall very decidedly into the former category. (He will later belch out smoke to create a night in which to hide himself (252-8): he fails in this attempt.) If Cacus is irredeemably evil, will that make it impossible to feel any sympathy for him when he becomes the victim – as soon happens?

Introduced by the epic title *Alcides* (descendant of Alceus), Hercules arrives at the scene. We are reminded that he, like Cacus, is a creature of violence. He is on his way back from Spain where he has killed the three-bodied monster Geryon and taken his cattle. But his violence is at the service of civilisation: he rids the world of monsters; he is a great avenger, and now a god (201). Cacus is wild, frenzied (*furiis*: think of the role of *furor* in the poem), an insatiable practitioner of crime and trickery (205-6).

The story that follows is also told by Livy in a passage given as an unseen in this book (see pp. 16-17). You may wish to compare the two accounts (we cannot be sure about which version was written first). Virgil's Cacus is far more alarming than Livy's. His trick of dragging the cattle into his cave by their tails – common to both accounts – is not without its cunning: it is taken from the god Hermes' theft of Apollo's cattle in the Homeric Hymn to Hermes (73-8). What do you feel about his trickery here? Evander's story moves forward vividly. The grandly polysyllabic patronymic *Amphitryoniades* ('son of Amphitryon') used of Hercules perhaps adds piquancy to the hero's puzzlement: intelligence was never his strong point! He cannot find the missing cattle and prepares to move on. But then, in lines resonant with long syllables (215-18), Virgil orchestrates the grove and the hills as the lowing cattle give Cacus' game away. In a sentence of fine rapidity – 219-21: note the dactylic 220 and the pluperfect *exarserat*: Hercules is enraged even before Virgil has informed us of the fact – the hero seizes his weapons and chases after Cacus. In a heavily spondaic line (222) we see the monster afraid. Then he gets a move on! Are you at all surprised at his panic and sudden flight?

And what do you feel about the fact that Hercules' anger blazes *furiis* and *atro felle*? If *furor* is something utterly bad in the poem, how can it be that the great civilising hero Hercules is possessed by it? This is something you will need to think about.

10. Cicero, *Pro Caelio* 31-80 (Pre-U from 2010 to 2012)

Pro Caelio 31-80

[33] sed tamen ex ipsa quaeram prius utrum me secum severe et graviter et prisce agere malit, an remisse et leniter et urbane. si illo austero more ac modo, aliquis mihi ab inferis excitandus est ex barbatis illis, non hac barbula qua ista delectatur, sed illa horrida quam in statuis antiquis atque imaginibus videmus, qui obiurget mulierem et qui pro me loquatur, ne mihi ista forte suscenseat. exsistat igitur ex hac ipsa familia aliquis ac potissimum Caecus ille; minimum enim dolorem capiet, qui istam non videbit. qui profecto, si exstiterit, sic aget ac sic loquetur: 'mulier, quid tibi cum Caelio, quid cum homine adulescentulo, quid cum alieno? cur aut tam familiaris huic fuisti, ut aurum commodares, aut tam inimica, ut venenum timeres? non patrem tuum videras, non patruum, non avum, non proavum, non abavum, non atavum audieras consules fuisse; [34] non denique modo te Q. Metelli matrimonium tenuisse sciebas, clarissimi ac fortissimi viri patriaeque amantissimi, qui simul ac pedem limine extulerat, omnes prope civis virtute, gloria, dignitate superabat? cum ex amplissimo genere in familiam clarissimam nupsisses, cur tibi Caelius tam coniunctus

fuit? cognatus, adfinis, viri tui familiaris? nihil eorum. quid igitur fuit nisi quaedam temeritas ac libido?

At the outset of his speech Cicero stresses that Caelius' trial is taking place during a public holiday. The games that are being held, the *ludi megalenses*, were *scenici* (dramatic), and it is thus a brilliant stroke of the orator's to import into his speech two character types familiar from Roman comedy. There is first the crustily conservative father of this excerpt and later the trendy young man whom Cicero represents in his portrayal of Clodius (36).[7]

The technical term for the 'speech in character' which Cicero gives to Appius Claudius Caecus (you will obviously wish to read all about him in the notes) is *prosôpopoiia*. Cicero's use of it here won admiration from ancient critics. It is introduced with tremendous aplomb. There is the absurd pretence that Clodia can have a say in who should address her. The sets of adverbs in the first sentence pit the grim old-style *mores* against the decadent urbanity of today. A jolly reference to necromancy leads to a disquisition on beards: the unkempt beards of the old days are set against the carefully trimmed beards of such men as Clodia's brother (see Austin's note). And the beards of yesteryear are given grandeur and dignity by the reference to sculpture: they have the permanence of stone. Finally, Cicero makes a splendid joke. Caecus is just the right ancestor to be summoned. Because he is blind he will not have to see his shameless descendant!

Cicero was famous for his sense of humour. When Caesar was fighting in Gaul, he used to wait impatiently for reports from Rome of his latest witticism. You may well wish to identify what makes this passage funny, both in the lead-in (we have already drawn attention to the joke about Caecus' blindness) and in the speech itself. You may also want to go beyond our passage to the end of 34 and respond to Caecus' indignation about the use which Clodia is making of his aqueduct and his road. And at the start of 35 what danger does Cicero think he might be running by introducing this censorious figure? (Caecus had been censor in 312 BC.) Cicero will have changed his tone to suit the character (Quintilian 11.1.39). How do you imagine that he played the part? What rhetorical features can you discover in the speech (tricolon, for example), and how do they contribute to its effect?[8] What do you think of the pile-up of words for ancestors in the sentence beginning *non patrem ...*?

However, beneath all the knock-about farce of the presentation, something very serious is going on. After all, this is not an unimportant matter for Caelius. What *are* the serious points about Clodia that Cicero is making in Caecus' speech? (Remember that she was suspected of having killed her husband.) Do you feel that the seriousness of the message is in any way undermined by the comic framework which Cicero employs to put it across?

---

[7] You may wish to see how Plautus handles these character types in say *Mostellaria* with Theopropides as the father and Philolaches as the son.

[8] *dignitate superabat* is one of Cicero's famous *clausulae* (i.e. one of his famous rhythms for ending a sentence). Perhaps he is identifying with Caecus!

5. Bibliographies

5. Bibliographies

This bibliography was compiled in April 2009. We have not included the editions of the texts specified by the examination boards.

Catullus
A first-class modern edition provides the most helpful (because literal and not unstylish) translation. This is John Godwin's *Catullus, Poems 61-68* and *Catullus, The Shorter Poems* (Aris and Phillips, Warminster, 1995 & 1999). His notes tackle Catullus' obscenity with a commendably unembarrassed frankness.

There is a vast quantity of modern literature on Catullus. One particularly enjoyable book is T.P. Wiseman's *Catullus and His World* (Cambridge, 1985). John Godwin's *Reading Catullus* (Bristol Phoenix Press, 2008) is recommended as well. It would also prove profitable to explore the splendid collection of essays in Marilyn B. Skinner (ed.), *A Companion to Catullus* (Blackwell, 2007). This gives an excellent conspectus of where Catullan criticism stands at the start of the twenty-first century. Julia Haig Gaisser (ed.), Oxford Readings in Classical Studies, *Catullus* (Oxford, 2007) offers a sampling of the most interesting work on Catullus from around 1950 to 2000, including Richard W. Hooper's 'In Defence of Catullus' Dirty Sparrow', a lively article about the possible double meaning of the word *passer.*

Cicero, *Pro Caelio*
The recommended translation is D.H. Berry's in *Cicero, Defence Speeches* in the Oxford World's Classics series (Oxford, 2001). It contains a good introduction, brief notes and a bibliography. Chapters 2 & 3 of T.P. Wiseman, *Catullus and His World, A Reappraisal* (Cambridge, 1985) provide illuminating background. T.A. Dorey, 'Cicero, Clodia, and the *Pro Caelio*', *Greece and Rome* 5 (1958), 175ff. is well worth tracking down. A.W. Lintott, *Cicero as Evidence* (Oxford, 2008) is also recommended (see the index 'M. Caelius Rufus' and especially Appendix 3 'Further Notes on the *Pro Caelio*'). There is a helpful and informative review of the book in the *Bryn Mawr Classical Review* (online publication) 2009-4-39.

On Cicero's oratory, the following are valuable: A.E. Douglas, *Cicero* (Oxford, 1968, 2nd edn 1979), James M. May, *Trials of Character: The Eloquence of Ciceronian Ethos* (North Carolina, 1988), R.G.M. Nisbet, 'The Speeches', chapter 3 in T.A. Dorey (ed.), *Cicero* (Routledge & Kegan Paul, London, 1965), Jonathan Powell and Jeremy Paterson, *Cicero the Advocate* (Oxford, 2004) (the introduction and Part 1 deal comprehensively with the law and oratory), Catherine Steel, *Roman Oratory* (Cambridge, 2006), Ann

Vasaly, *Representations: Images of the World in Ciceronian Oratory* (California, 1993). On the whole oratorical tradition, see George A. Kennedy, *A New History of Classical Rhetoric* (Princeton, 1994).

R.G. Austin's edition (prescribed for Pre-U) of *Pro Caelio* (3rd edn Oxford, 1960) is outstanding.

Livy 23

There is a good modern translation of this book in Livy, *Hannibal's War, Books 21-30* (Oxford World's Classics, 2006). This has a fairly short introduction and helpful but not very copious notes by Dexter Hoyos, and a useful glossary and index. Good general books on Livy are T.A. Dorey (ed.), *Livy* (London, 1971) (a collection of essays), P.G. Walsh, *Livy: His Historical Aims and Methods* (Cambridge, 1963, 2nd edn Bristol Classical Press, 1989) (still valuable), and T.J. Luce, *Livy: The Composition of His History* (Princeton, 1977). There is an excellent chapter on Livy in C.S. Kraus and A.J. Woodman, *Latin Historians* (Oxford, 1997).

A good modern book on the Punic Wars is A. Goldsworthy, *The Punic Wars* (London, 2000; reissued in paperback as *The Fall of Carthage: The Punic Wars*, 2003) .

Propertius

The recommended verse translation is Guy Lee's *Propertius: The Poems* (Oxford, 1994) of which the *Bryn Mawr Classical Review* wrote, 'Lee's translation of P. is not bold or sparkling or avant-garde. It is something much more difficult and desirable than that – an honest attempt at a quietly accurate and reliable version made by a highly sensitive scholar.' Workmanlike prose translations are given in G.P. Goold's Loeb *Propertius* (1990, revised 1999) and Heyworth's *Cynthia* (see below). It is unfortunately the case that the two most recent books on the poet are inappropriate for the demands of A2. Francis Cairns, *Sextus Propertius: The Augustan Elegist* (Cambridge, 2006) is an impressive work of scholarship but is too concerned with technical minutiae and possible patronage to develop a useful picture of the poet as a whole, while Alison Keith's *Propertius: Poet of Love and Leisure* (Duckworth, 2008) is overly and reductively theoretical, though it does contain illuminating passages, and even her copious quotations fail to give an impression of the centrality of Cynthia in the poet's work.

The edition of Book 3 by S.J. Heyworth and J. Morwood (Oxford, 2010) has a substantial introduction which deals with the fundamental issues. It also contains copious notes. Heyworth's *Cynthia* offers full discussion of textual matters (Oxford, 2007, now in paperback). Maria Wyke's *The Roman Mistress* (Oxford, 2002) offers an interesting exploration of the way in which the male poet writes about his elegiac girlfriend. M. Hubbard, *Propertius* (Duckworth, 1974) remains sound and still has interesting things to say.

Other books worth trying to track down are are S. Commager, *A Prolegomenon to Propertius* Oklahoma, 1974) and H.-P. Stahl, *Propertius: 'Love' and 'War', Individual and State Under Augustus* (California, 1985).

Sallust

The recommended translation is the new Penguin Classic by A.J. Woodman, *Sallust, Catiline's War, The Jugurthine War, Histories* (2007) with introduction and notes. A helpful commentary is J.T. Ramsey's *Sallust's Bellum Catilinae* (American Philological Association, Oxford, rev. edn 2007). For the 2007 revision Ramsey has provided several additional resources: the complete Latin text in either PDF (formatted to the print volume) or Word (adjustable and formattable to suit the reader's wishes) format, as well as PDFs of a 'who's who' of persons mentioned in the text, and a page of supplementary bibliography of current work. These items are most conveniently available now at http://www.oup.com/us/companion.websites/9780195320855/?view=usa but are also available through the American Philological Association.

A good historical and literary study is A.T. Wilkins, *Villain or Hero: Sallust's Portrayal of Catiline* (Peter Lang, New York, 1994). John Murrell's excellent *Cicero and the Roman Republic* (Cambridge, 2008) sets the Catiline episode in context. Further useful background can be found in P.A. Brunt, *Social Conflicts in the Roman Republic* (London, 1971), 124-32 (user-friendly for students), Erich S. Gruen, *The Last Generation of the Roman Republic* (California, 1974), 416-33, and Peter Wiseman, 'The Peasants' Revolt and the Bankrupts' Plot' in *Cambridge Ancient History* 9, 346-58. Andrew R. Dyck's admirable edition of Cicero's *Catilinarians* (Cambridge, 2008) is also recommended.

Good writing on Sallust can be found in: C.S. Kraus and A.J. Woodman, *Latin Historians* (Oxford, 1997), J. Marincola (ed.), *A Companion to Greek and Roman Historiography* (Blackwell, 2007) and A, Geldherr (ed.), *The Cambridge Companion to Roman Historiography* (Cambridge, 2008). The only book in English which is devoted to Sallust and his work is *Sallust* by the acknowledged master of the period, Sir Ronald Syme. This was first published in 1964 and reissued by the University of California Press with a new Foreword by R. Mellor in 2002.

Tacitus, *Annals* 14 and 15

A note of caution should be sounded over translations of the *Annals*. A.J. Woodman's for Indianapolis and Cambridge (2004) is perhaps somewhat eccentric since it attempts to reproduce the flavour of Tacitus' distinctive Latin style in its English. However, it is to be vastly preferred to Michael Grant's (Penguin, 1956, reprinted with a new bibliography in 1989).

A valuable book of excerpts from Tacitus' work which will enable these two books to be set in context is Christopher Burnand, *Tacitus and Imperial Rome* (Cambridge, 2010).

Good general books on Tacitus are Rhiannon Ash, *Tacitus* (Bristol Classical

Press, 2006), R. Martin, *Tacitus* (London 1981, revised 1994) and R. Syme, *Tacitus* (2 vols, Oxford, 1958) (the classic in the field by an unparalleled expert). There is an excellent chapter on Tacitus in C.S. Kraus and A.J. Woodman, *Latin Historians* (Oxford, 1997).

The best book for establishing the historical context of these books is Miriam T. Griffin, *Nero: The End of a Dynasty* (London, Batsford, 1984).

On the *Annals*: B. Walker, *The Annals of Tacitus* (Manchester, 1952) (a very good introduction which has lasted well).

There is a good essay on Book 15.36-7 in A.J. Woodman, *Tacitus Reviewed* (Oxford, 1998).

Virgil, *Aeneid* 1, 4 and 8

The recommended prose translation is that by D.A. West (Penguin, 1991).

A good Latin text is set opposite a fairly literal prose translation in the Loeb edition by H. Rushton Fairclough, revised by G.P. Goold (Harvard, 1999).

K.W. Gransden's *Virgil in English* (Penguin, 1996) is an excellent anthology of selections from English translations and versions of the poet from Chaucer to Seamus Heaney. A helpful book for setting the three books in the context of Virgil's work as a whole as well as in the *Aeneid* is J. Morwood, *Virgil: A Poet in Augustan Rome* (Cambridge, 2008) (selections in English with commentary from all of the poet's work).

Excellent editions of these books are those by R.G. Austin of 1 and 4 (Oxford, 1971, 1955 respectively) and by K.W. Gransden of 8 (Cambridge, 1976). R.D. Williams' edition of the whole of the *Aeneid* (London, 1972-3, reprinted by Bristol Classical Press) is a masterpiece of concision and clarity. K. Maclennan's *Virgil: Aeneid 4* (Bristol Classical Press, 2007) is aimed at schools, and a brilliant success.

Select Virgil bibliography

F. Cairns, *Virgil's Augustan Epic* (Cambridge, 1989). A optimistic reading of the poem.

W.A. Camps, *An Introduction to Virgil's Aeneid* (Oxford, 1969). Still the best introduction to the poet.

S. Commager (ed.), *Virgil: A Collection of Critical Essays* (Englewood Cliffs NJ, 1966). A useful collection of classic articles.

D.C. Feeney, *The Gods in Epic* (Oxford, 1991) chapters 3-4. The gods of the poem are seen as anthropomorphic fictional characters in the Homeric tradition; they do not simply mirror the deities of Roman religion.

K.W. Gransden, *Virgil, The Aeneid* (2nd edn by S.J. Harrison) (Cambridge, 2004). A serviceable *vade mecum*, but written on a smaller scale than the Camps and Williams equivalents. Harrison's bibliography is extremely helpful.

J. Griffin, 'The Creation of Characters in the Aeneid', in B.K. Gold (ed.),

5. Bibliographies

Literature and Artistic Patronage in Ancient Rome (Texas, 1982), 118-34, or in his *Latin Poetry and Roman Life* (Duckworth, 1986).

J. Griffin, *Virgil* (Oxford, 1986). A brief but elegant and perceptive introduction.

P. Hardie, *Virgil* (*Greece and Rome, New Surveys* 28, Oxford 1998). A magisterial and highly readable survey of where Virgil studies stood at the very end of the twentieth century.

P. Hardie, *Virgil's Aeneid: Cosmos and Imperium* (Oxford, 1986): see review by J. Griffin, *JRS* 78 (1988). An optimistic reading of the poem, seeing it as working in harmony with the monarchical ideology of Augustus.

P. Hardie (ed.), *Virgil: Critical Assessments of Classical Authors*, 4 vols (London, 1999). Reprinted and translated articles.

S.J. Harrison (ed.), *Oxford Reading's in Vergil's Aeneid* (Oxford, 1990). A fine collection of essays, it contains an excellent scholarly survey by the editor of the scholarship on the poem since 1900.

R. Heinze, *Virgil's Epic Technique* (originally published in German, 1903; Eng. tr. Bristol, 1993). A classic, it deals with the way Virgil worked within the literary tradition which he inherited and is responsive to the drama and pathos in the action and characterization of the poem.

N.M. Horsfall (ed.), *A Companion to the study of Virgil* (Leiden, 1995). Traditional in outlook and focused on key questions.

R.H.A. Jenkyns, *Classical Epic: Homer and Virgil* (Bristol Classical Press, 1992). Thoughtful and useful.

R.H.A. Jenkyns, *Virgil's Experience: Nature and History, Names, and Places* (Oxford, 1998). Stimulating and wide-ranging, if eschewing modernist approaches to the poet.

W.R. Johnson, *Darkness Visible* (Berkeley, 1976). A pessimistic reading of the poem, this is at times eccentric but certainly proves stimulating.

R.O.A.M. Lyne, *Further Voices in Virgil's Aeneid* (Oxford, 1987). The 'further voices' subvert the outwardly positive epic story.

C.A. Martindale (ed.), *The Cambridge Companion to Virgil* (Cambridge, 1997). The essays here prove a good launching-off point for the modern debate on the poet; there is a strong emphasis on his reception.

A. Rossi, *Contexts of War: Manipulation of Genre in Virgilian Battle Narrative* (Ann Arbor, 2003): see review in *Bryn Mawr Classical Review* (on line publication) 2004 (11)).

H.-P. Stahl (ed.), *Virgil's Aeneid: Augustan Epic and Political Context* (Leiden, 1998).

G. Williams, *Technique and Ideas in the Aeneid* (Yale, 1983). This includes interesting writing on the gods who are seen as tropes for human motivation and authorial manipulation.

R.D. Williams, *The Aeneid* (2nd edn, with an introduction by J. Morwood, Bristol Classical Press, 2009). The summation of a lifetime's work on the poem.

6. Unseen Literary Criticism Exercises

1. A lover's jealousy

Horace writes about Lydia's new love affair.

cum tu, Lydia, Telephi
cervicem roseam, cerea Telephi
   laudas bracchia, vae, meum
fervens difficili bile tumet iecur.

tunc nec mens mihi nec color
certa sede manet, umor et in genas   5
   furtim labitur, arguens
quam lentis penitus macerer ignibus.

uror, seu tibi candidos
turparunt umeros inmodicae mero   10
   rixae, sive puer furens
inpressit memorem dente labris notam.

non, si me satis audias,
speres perpetuum dulcia barbare
   laedentem oscula, quae Venus   15
quinta parte sui nectaris imbuit.

felices ter et amplius
quos inrupta tenet copula nec malis
   divulsus querimoniis
suprema citius solvet amor die.   20

Horace, *Odes* 1.13

1. A lover's jealousy

When you praise Telephus' rosy neck, Lydia, Telephus' wax-like arms, ah! my seething liver swells with angry bile. Then neither my mind nor my colour remains in its fixed seat, and moisture furtively slips onto my cheeks, showing by what slow fires I am tormented deep inside. I am on fire, whether quarrels immoderate with wine have scarred your white shoulders or the frenzied lad has left with his tooth on your lips a mark to remember him by. If you would listen enough to me, you wouldn't hope that he will be yours for ever, barbarously wounding those sweet kisses which Venus has imbued with the quintessence of her nectar. Thrice happy, and more, are those whom an unbroken bond holds, and whom a love torn asunder by wicked quarrels will not sever sooner than their final day.

(a) What picture does this poem paint of the love between Lydia and Telephus? You should make close reference to the language used. [6]
(b) How does Horace emphasise, through his use of language, his own pain? [10]
(c) Printed below is David West's translation of lines 9-12. Compare this with the translation above and explain which you think captures better the spirit and meaning of the Latin. [4]

> I burn if drunken
> brawls sully your white shoulder
> or if that wild boy's tooth
> prints the tell-tale mark upon your lips.

125

2. Hannibal

Hannibal, the great Carthaginian leader, famously led his army, elephants and all, over the wintry Alps into Italy and all the way to Rome itself. The Romans fought a war of attrition and, in the end, a lack of supplies and of support from the Italian people compelled Hannibal to retreat back to Carthage where he fought and lost the decisive battle against Scipio at Zama. He was later forced to flee Carthage and live as a refugee, first in Syria, then Bithynia.

expende Hannibalem: quot libras in duce summo
invenies? hic est quem non capit Africa Mauro
percussa oceano Niloque admota tepenti
rursus ad Aethiopum populos aliosque elephantos.
additur imperiis Hispania, Pyrenaeum   5
transilit. opposuit natura Alpemque nivemque:
diducit scopulos et montem rumpit <u>aceto</u>.
iam tenet Italiam, tamen ultra pergere tendit.
'acti' inquit 'nihil est, nisi Poeno milite portas
frangimus et media vexillum pono <u>Subura</u>.'   10
o qualis facies et quali digna tabella,
cum <u>Gaetula</u> ducem portaret belua luscum!
exitus ergo quis est? o gloria! vincitur idem
nempe et in exsilium praeceps fugit atque ibi magnus
mirandusque cliens sedet ad praetoria regis,   15
donec <u>Bithyno</u> libeat vigilare <u>tyranno</u>.
finem animae, quae res humanas miscuit olim,
non gladii, non saxa dabunt nec tela, sed ille
<u>Cannarum</u> vindex et tanti sanguinis ultor
<u>anulus</u>. i, demens, et saevas curre per Alpes   20
ut pueris placeas et declamatio fias.

Juvenal, *Satires* 10.147-67

aceto – vinegar. (Livy tells how Hannibal broke his way through a seemingly impassable section of the Alps by heating the rocks which blocked the way and then shattering them with old wine which had turned into vinegar.)

Subura – a central district in Rome.

Gaetula – Gaetulian (= African).

Bithyno … tyranno: the Bithynian tyrant was Prusias I; after harbouring Hannibal for several years, he was persuaded to hand him over to the Romans. Hannibal escaped this fate by committing suicide.

Cannarum: Cannae was the site of one of Hannibal's most successful battles in Italy.

anulus: when Hannibal committed suicide he used poison hidden in a ring.

Weigh Hannibal. How many pounds will you find in the great general? This is he whom Africa cannot contain, Africa beaten by the Moorish sea and reaching the warm Nile southward to the Ethiopian peoples and the other kind of elephant. Spain is added to his empires, and he leaps across the Pyrenees. Nature set both the Alps and snow in his path: he splits the rocks and shatters the mountain with vinegar. Now he holds Italy, but persists in pressing further. 'Nothing has been achieved,' he says, 'unless we break down the gates with Punic soldiery and I plant my banner in mid-Subura.' O what a sight, and worthy of what a picture, when the Gaetulian beast carried the one-eyed leader! So, what is his end? What glory! The very same man is, of course, defeated, flees headlong into exile, and there sits, a great and wonderful client, at the king's palace, until it please the Bithynian tyrant to awake. To the soul which once turned human affairs upside down not swords will give an end, not stones or spears, but that avenger of Cannae and of so much blood, a ring. Go, madman, and run over the cruel Alps, just to entertain children and become the subject of a speech.

(a) How does Juvenal emphasise the extent of Hannibal's achievements? In your answer you should make close reference to the Latin used. [10]
(b) Where or what is the satire here? Support your answer with close reference to the Latin. [6]
(c) Printed below is a much freer translation of lines 20-1. Compare this with the version above and explain which you think captures better the spirit and meaning of the Latin. [4]

Hannibal, you're mad: the Alps are bad but go on, run about.
You're sure to please the school boys and make the poets shout.

3. The nature of love

Propertius discusses the nature of love and explains why it is appropriate to portray love as a boy.

quicumque ille fuit, puerum qui pinxit Amorem,
　　nonne putas miras hunc habuisse manus?
is primum vidit sine sensu vivere amantis,
　　et levibus curis magna perire bona.
idem non frustra ventosas addidit alas,　　　　　　　　　　5
　　fecit et humano corde volare deum:
scilicet alterna quoniam iactamur in unda,
　　nostraque non ullis permanet aura locis.
et merito hamatis manus est armata sagittis,
　　et pharetra ex umero Cnosia utroque iacet:　　　　　　　10
ante ferit quoniam, tuti quam cernimus hostem,
　　nec quisquam ex illo vulnere sanus abit.
in me tela manent, manet et puerilis imago:
　　sed certe pennas perdidit ille suas;
evolat heu nostro quoniam de pectore nusquam,　　　　　15
　　assiduusque meo sanguine bella gerit.
quid tibi iucundum est siccis habitare medullis?
　　si pudor est, alio traice tela una!

Propertius 2.12.1-18

128

3. The nature of love

Whoever he was who painted Love as a boy, do you not think he had a marvellous touch? He first saw that lovers live without good sense, and that great estates are destroyed by little desires. The same man added, not without reason, wings that mimic the wind, and made the god fly in the human heart, presumably since we are tossed on fluctuating waves: the breeze nowhere remains steady in our favour. And rightly is his hand armed with barbed arrows, and a Cretan quiver lies on his two shoulders, since he strikes us first, when we feel safe, before we see the enemy, and no one goes off unscathed from that wound.

In my case the weapons remain valid; so too does the boyish appearance; but he has certainly lost his wings, since (alas!) he nowhere flies off from our heart, and constantly wages war in my life-blood. Why is it pleasing for you to inhabit my dried out marrow? If you have any shame, direct your weapons elsewhere.

Trans. S.J. Heyworth

(a) Lines 1-4 (*quicumque ... bona*): have these lines been well translated in the version above? In your answer you should give examples of meaning or poetic effects which have been conveyed well or lost in translation. [4]

(b) Lines 13-18 (*in me ... una*): what do you think these lines tell us about the poet, his feelings and the object of his love? Support your answer with close reference to the Latin used. [6]

(c) Overall, is this poem a positive portrayal of love? Explain your answer with close reference to the Latin used. [10]

129

4. Tartarus

*Aeneas has descended to the Underworld to meet the ghost of his father.
As he journeys through the realms of the dead he sees the
entrance to Tartarus, the classical hell.*

constitit Aeneas strepitumque exterritus hausit.
'quae scelerum facies? o virgo, effare; quibusve
urgentur poenis? quis tantus plangor ad auras?'
tum vates sic orsa loqui: 'dux inclute Teucrum,
nulli fas casto sceleratum insistere limen;   5
sed me cum lucis Hecate praefecit Avernis,
ipsa deum poenas docuit perque omnia duxit.
Cnosius haec Rhadamanthus habet durissima regna
castigatque auditque dolos subigitque fateri
quae quis apud superos furto laetatus inani   10
distulit in seram commissa piacula mortem.
continuo sontes ultrix accincta flagello
<u>Tisiphone</u> quatit insultans, torvosque sinistra
intentans angues vocat agmina saeva sororum.
tum demum horrisono stridentes cardine sacrae   15
panduntur portae. cernis custodia qualis
vestibulo sedeat, facies quae limina servet?
quinquaginta atris immanis hiatibus Hydra
saevior intus habet sedem. tum Tartarus ipse
bis patet in praeceps tantum tenditque sub umbras   20
quantus ad aetherium caeli suspectus Olympum.
hic genus antiquum Terrae, <u>Titania pubes</u>,
fulmine deiecti fundo volvuntur in imo.

Virgil, *Aeneid* 6.559-81

Tisiphone – Tisiphone was one of the Furies (the terrifying spirits of revenge).
Titania pubes – the Titans, born from the Earth, were an ancient race of
   demi-gods who, beaten in a battle against the Olympian gods, were cast into
   Tartarus by them.

Aeneas stopped and terrified he took in the din. 'What kind of crimes are here? O maiden, tell me; or by what punishments are they pressed? What great wailing is this that reaches the upper air?' Then the prophetess thus began to speak: 'Oh famous leader of the Trojans, it is not permitted for any righteous person to stand upon the threshold of the wicked; but when Hecate put me in charge of the groves of Avernus, she told me of the gods' punishments and explained everything. Cretan Rhadamanthus rules these most harsh realms and he chastises and listens to deceits and forces men to confess the crimes which, committed in the world above, any of them, delighting in empty deceit has put off too late until death. Without pause avenging Tisiphone, girded with her whip, leaping upon them beats the guilty, and stretching out with her left hand her grim snakes she calls up the savage ranks of her sisters. Then at last, creaking on their screeching hinges, the cursed gates are opened. Do you see what sort of sentry sits in the entrance way, what kind of shape watches over the threshold? Hydra, monstrous with her fifty yawning black jaws, still more savage has her home within. Then Tartarus itself reveals a sheer abyss and stretches into the shades twice as far as the view of heaven reaches up to airy Olympus. Here Earth's ancient offspring, the Titan race, cast down by a thunderbolt, roll about on the lowest plane of the world.

(a) Lines 1-3 (*constitit … auras*): what poetic effects are there here
    which are lost in the translation offered above?   [4]
(b) Lines 1-7 (*constitit … duxit*): what atmosphere is created here?
    Explain your answer by close reference to the Latin used.   [6]
(c) Lines 8-23 (*Cnosius … imo*): how is Tartarus made to seem
    absolutely terrifying?   [10]

5. The simple life

Tibullus praises the delights of simple country living.

divitias alius fulvo sibi congerat auro
    et teneat culti iugera multa soli,
quem labor adsiduus vicino terreat hoste,
    martia cui somnos classica pulsa fugent:
me mea paupertas vita traducat inerti,   5
    dum meus adsiduo luceat igne focus.
ipse seram teneras maturo tempore vites
    rusticus et facili grandia poma manu;
nec spes destituat, sed frugum semper acervos
    praebeat et pleno pinguia musta lacu.   10
nam veneror, seu stipes habet desertus in agris
    seu vetus in trivio florida serta lapis,
et quodcumque mihi pomum novus educat annus,
    libatum agricolae ponitur ante deo.
flava Ceres, tibi sit nostro de rure corona   15
    spicea, quae templi pendeat ante fores,
pomosisque ruber custos ponatur in hortis,
    terreat ut saeva falce Priapus aves.
vos quoque, felicis quondam, nunc pauperis agri
    custodes, fertis munera vestra, Lares.   20

Tibullus 1

Ceres – a goddess of agriculture, and associated with corn in particular.
Priapus – the well-endowed god of gardens and vineyards.
Lares – the gods of the household who watched over its well-being.

5. The simple life

Let someone else heap up for himself riches in yellow gold and hold many acres of cultivated soil. Let constant toil terrify him as the enemy is near, let the blast of the War god's trumpet put his sleep to flight: as for me, may my poverty lead me on in a stress-free life, provided that my hearth shines with a constant fire. I myself, a rustic, shall plant tender vines at the right time and big apple trees with an easy hand; and may my hope not let me down, but may it always provide me with heaps of produce and the rich juice of the vine in a full vat. For I show reverence, whether an isolated tree-trunk in the fields has my garlands of flowers or an old stone at a crossroads, and whatever fruit the new year brings forth for me is offered and set forth for the god of the farmer. Yellow Ceres, may you have a garland of corn from our countryside and may it hang before the doors of your temple, and may a red guard be put in the orchards so that Priapus can terrify the birds with his savage scythe. And you also carry your gifts, guardians of our once prosperous, now poor land, Lares.

(a) *divitias ... manu* (lines 1-8): how does Tibullus make the simple life seem attractive? [10]

(b) *ipse seram ... Lares* (lines 7-20): how and why does Tibullus worship the gods? In your answer you should refer closely to the Latin and explain how his use of language conveys the meaning. [6]

(c) Do you agree with the translation offered for *inerti* (line 5), *facili* (line 8) and *felicis* (line 19)? Explain your answer. [4]

133

Appendix:
Prose Composition Vocabulary

Appendix
Prose Composition Vocabulary

able, I am	**possum, posse, potui**
about	**circa** + accusative
absent	**absens, absentis**
absolute	**infinitus, -a, -um**
accompany	**comitor** (1)
(on) account of	**ob** + accusative
accustomed, I am	**soleo, -ere, solitus sum**
acquit	**solvo, -ere, solvi, solutum**
act	**ago, -ere, egi, actum; facio, -ere, feci, factum**
admit	**fateor, -eri, fassus sum**
advance	**progredior -i, progressus sum**
advice	**consilium, -ii** n
advise	**moneo** (2)
Africa	**Africa, -ae** f
again	**iterum**
all	**omnis, -e**
alone	**solus, -a, -um**
always	**semper**
among	**inter** + accusative
and	**et, atque (ac), -que**
and not	**neque (nec)**
and yet	**atqui**
anger	**ira, -ae** f
angry	**iratus, -a, -um**
I am angry	**irascor, -i, iratus sum**
anyone	**quisquam; quis**
Apollo	**Apollo, -inis** m
appropriate	**idoneus, -a, -um**
arise	**orior, -iri, ortus sum**
armed men	**armati, -orum** m pl
arms, armour	**arma, -orum** n pl
army	**exercitus, -us** m
arrest	**comprehendo, -ere, -prehendi, -prehensum**
arrive	**advenio, -ire, -veni, -ventum ad** + accusative
arrogance	**superbia, -ae** f
arrow	**sagitta, -ae** f
Arruns	**Arruns, -untis** m
as follows	**sic**
as if	**quasi; velut si**
ask	**rogo** (1)
at last	**tandem**
attack	**oppugno** (1); **adorior, -iri, adortus sum**

attend to	**curo** (1)
bar	**obsero** (1)
battle	**proelium, -ii** n
be	**sum, esse, fui**
be present	**adsum, -esse, -fui**
beast of burden	**iumentum, -i** n
because	**quod; quia**
because of	**propter** + accusative
bed	**lectus, -i** m
before (*adverb*)	**antea**
before (*conjunction*)	**antequam; priusquam**
beg	**oro** (1)
beg for	**imploro** (1)
begin	**coepi, -isse; incipio, -ere, -cepi, -ceptum**
believe	**credo, -ere, credidi, creditum** + dative
betroth	**despondeo, -ere, -spondi, -sponsum**
bind	**vincio, -ire, vinxi, vinctum**
bird	**avis, -is** f
birth, by	**natu**
bodyguard	**stipator, -oris** m
bow (the head)	**demitto, -ere, -misi, -missum**
brave	**fortis, -e**
break down	**effringo, -ere, -fregi, -fractum**
bring (a person)	**(ad)duco, -ere, -xi, -ctum**
brother	**frater, fratris,** m
Brutus	**Brutus, -i** m
build	**aedifico** (1)
but	**sed**
but … not	**nec tamen**
Caesar	**Caesar, -aris** m
call	**voco** (1)
call away	**avoco** (1)
call together	**convoco** (1)
call upon (by name)	**appello** (1)
camp	**castra, -orum** n pl
carry	**fero, ferre, tuli, latum; porto** (1)
Carthage	**Carthago, -inis** f
Carthaginians	**Carthaginienses, -ium** m pl; **Poeni, -orum** m pl
cavalryman	**eques, -itis** m
(a) certain	**quidam, quaedam, quoddam**
certainly	**certe**
chain	**vinculum, -i** n; **catena, -ae** f
chance, by	**forte**
charge	**impetus, -us** m
check, hold in check	**reprimo, -ere, -pressi, -pressum**
citadel	**arx, arcis** f

citizen	**civis, -is** m
city	**urbs, urbis** f
Clearchus	**Clearchus, -i** m
clever	**ingeniosus, -a, -um**
cloak	**paludamentum, -i** n
clothes	**vestimenta, -orum** n pl
colleague	**collega, -ae** m
column	**columna, -ae** f
come	**venio, -ire, veni, ventum**
come forth, out	**prodeo, -ire, -ii, -itum**
comfort	**confirmo** (1)
commander	**imperator, -oris** m
common, shared	**communis, -e**
companion	**comes, -itis** m
compel	**cogo, -ere, coegi, coactum**
complain	**queror, -i, questus sum**
confident, I am	**pro certo habeo** (2)
conqueror	**victor, -oris** m
conspiracy	**coniuratio, ionis** f
conspirator	**coniuratus, -i** m
consult	**consulo, -ere, -sului, -sultum**
converse	**colloquor, -i, collocutus sum**
cook	**coquo, -ere, coxi, coctum**
country, fatherland	**patria, -ae** f
courage	**virtus, -utis** f
cruelty	**crudelitas, -atis** f
cry	**clamo** (1); **exclamo** (1)
customary	**solitus, -a, -um**
Curio	**Curio, -ionis** m
cut off	**deseco, -are, -ui, -ctum**
dagger	**pugio, -ionis** m
dangerous	**periculosus, -a, -um**
dare	**audeo, -ere, ausus sum**
daughter	**filia, ae** f
dawn, at	**prima luce**
day	**dies, diei** m
dear	**carus, -a, -um**
deception	**dolus, -i** m; **fraus, -dis** f
decide	**constituo, -ere, constitui, constitutum**
declare	**adfirmo** (1)
deed	**factum, -i** n; **facinus, -oris** n (especially of an evil deed)
defeat	**vinco, -ere, vici, victum**
delay (*noun*)	**mora, -ae** f
delay (*verb*)	**moror** (1)
Delphi	**Delphi, -orum** m pl
demand	**posco, -ere, poposci; flagito** (1)
deny	**nego** (1)

depart	**discedo, -ere, -cessi, -cessum**
descendants	**posteri, -orum** m pl
despair	**desperatio, -ionis** f
destroy	**deleo, -ere, -evi, -etum**
dinner	**cena, -ae** f
disaster	**clades, -is** f
discover	**cognosco, -ere, cognovi, cognitum**
disease	**morbus, -i** m; **pestis, -is** f
deserved	**dignus, -a, -um**
Diviciacus	**Diviciacus, -i** m
divine	**divinus, -a, -um**
do	**facio, -ere feci, factum**
door	**ianua, -ae** f; **foris, -is** f (*usually in plural*)
draw (a sword)	**stringo, -ere, strinxi, strictum**
drive	**ago, -ere, egi, actum**
drive back	**repello, -ere, reppuli, repulsum**
earth	**terra, -ae** f
easy	**facilis, -e**
either...or	**aut...aut**
emperor	**princeps, -ipis** m
encourage	**hortor** (1); **confirmo** (1)
enemy	**hostis, -is** m
enough	**satis**
Ennius	**Ennius, -ii** m
enquire for	**quaero, -ere, quaesivi, quaesitum**
enter	**ineo, -ire, -ii, -itum; ingredior, -i, -gressus sum; intro** (1)
escape	**effugio, -ere, -fugi, -fugitum**
even	**etiam**
execute	**supplicio adficio, -ere, -feci, -fectum**
exile	**exsilium, -ii** n
exstinguish	**exstinguo, -ere, -nxi, -nctum**
face to face	**coram**
fall	**cado, -ere, cecidi, casum**
fall down	**prolabor, -i, -lapsus sum**
famous	**praeclarus, -a, -um**
far	**procul**
father	**pater, patris** m
fatherland	**patria, -ae** f
fear, am afraid	**timeo** (2)
fear (*noun*)	**timor, -oris** m
few	**pauci, -ae, -a**
fiancé	**sponsus, -i** m
find	**invenio, -ire, -veni, -ventum**
find out, learn	**cognosco, -ere, -novi, -nitum**
first	**primus, -a, -um**
fight (*noun*)	**pugna, -ae** f

fight (*verb*)	**pugno** (1)
finish off	**conficio, -ere, -feci, -fectum**
fire	**ignis, -is** m
flee	**fugio, -ere, fugi, fugitum**
flight	**fuga, -ae** f
flower	**flos, floris** m
food	**cibus, -i** m
fool, deceive	**decipio, -ere, -cepi, -ceptum**
for	**nam**; **enim** (2nd word)
foundation	**fundamentum, -i** n
friend	**amicus, -i** m
from	**e/ex** + abl; **a/ab** + abl.
frighten	**terreo** (2)
further, furthermore	**praeterea**
Gabii	**Gabii, -iorum** m pl
Gabini	**Gabini, -orum** m pl
Gaius	**Gaius, Gaii** m
gain	**adipiscor, -i, adeptus sum**
garden	**hortus, -i** m
gate	**porta, -ae** f
gather	**colligo, -ere, -legi, -lectum**
gaze at	**intueor, -eri, -tuitus sum**
general	**imperator, -oris** m
German	**Germanus, -a, -um**
give	**do, dare, dedi, datum**
go	**eo, ire, i(v)i, itum**
go away	**abeo, -ire, -ii, -itum**; **discedo, -ere, -cessi, -cessum**
go forward	**progredior, -i, progressus sum**
go out	**exeo, -ire, -ii, -itum**
god	**deus, -i** m
great	**magnus, -a, -um**
Greek	**Graecus, -a, -um**
greet	**saluto** (1)
grief	**dolor, -oris** m
ground	**terra, -ae** f
hand over	**trado, -ere, tradidi, traditum**
head	**caput, -itis** n
head, make for	**peto, -ere, petivi, petitum**
hear	**audio** (4)
heart	*use* **pectus, -oris** n
here	**hic**
from here	**hinc**
help (*noun*)	**auxilium, -ii** n
help (*verb*)	**(ad)iuvo, -are, iuvi, iutum**
come to help	**subvenio, -ire, -veni, -ventum** + dative; **succurro, -ere, -curri, -cursum** + dative

hide	**celo** (1)
hill	**collis, -is** m
home	**domus, -us** f
hope	**spes, -ei** f
horse	**equus, -i** m
Hostius	**Hostius, -ii** m
housemaid	**ancilla, -ae** f
how big?	**quantus, -a, -um**
however	**tamen** (2nd word)
hunger	**fames, -is** f
if	**si**
but if	**sin (autem); quodsi**
ignorant	**ignarus, -a, -um**
immediately	**statim**
impudent	**impudens, -entis**
indeed	**vero**
infantryman	**pedes, -itis** m
influence	**auctoritas, -atis** f
inside, at home	**intus**
inspect	**inspicio, -ere, -spexi, -spectum**
intend	**in animo habeo** (2)
into	**in** + accusative
join	**iungo, -ere, iunxi, iunctum**
join battle	**proelium committo, -ere, -misi, -missum**
joy	**gaudium, -ii** n
journey	**iter, itineris** n
journey-money	**viaticum, -i** n
Junius	**Iunius, -ii** m
Jupiter	**Iuppiter, Iovis** m
just	**iustus, -a, -um**
kill	**interficio -ere, -feci, -fectum**
kind	**benignus, -a, -um**
king	**rex, regis** m
kiss (*verb*)	**osculor** (1)
kiss (*noun*)	**osculum, -i** n
knock (a door)	**pulso** (1)
lack	**careo** (2) + ablative
last, final	**ultimus, -a, -um**
at last	**tandem**
lead	**duco, -ere, duxi, ductum**
lead back	**reduco,** etc
leader	**dux, ducis** m
leading citizen	**princeps, -ipis** m

142

leave (= abandon)	**relinquo, -ere, reliqui, relictum**; (= depart) **discedo, -ere, -cessi, -cessum**
lictor	**lictor, -oris** m
lie	**iaceo** (2)
lie, tell lies	**mentior** (4)
life	**vita, -ae** f
lose	**perdo, -ere, perdidi, perditum; amitto, -ere, -misi, -missum**
loud	**magnus, -a, -um**
love	**amo** (1)
majority, the	**plerique, -aeque, -aque**
make,	**facio, -ere, feci, factum**
man	**vir, -i** m; **homo, -inis** m
Manlius	**Manlius, -ii** m
of Manlius	**Manlianus, -a, -um**
many	**multi, -ae, -a**
Marius	**Marius, -ii** m
master	**dominus, -i** m
matter	**res, rei** f
maiden	**virgo, -inis** f
mean	**significo** (1)
meanwhile	**interea, interim**
meet	**obviam eo, ire, i(v)i, itum** + dative
memorial	**monumentum, -i** n
messenger	**nuntius, -ii** m
midday	**meridies, -ei** m
middle	**medius, -a, -um**
mild	**mollis, -e**
military	**militaris, -e**
military matters	**res militaris, rei -is** f
Minturnae	**Minturnae, -arum** f pl
morning, in the	**mane**
mortal	**mortalis, -e**
mother	**mater, matris** f
move	**moveo, -ere, movi, motum**
name	**nomen, -inis** n
nearby	(adj.) **proximus, -a, -um**
neighbouring	**vicinus, -a, -um**
neither ... nor	**neque (nec)...neque (nec)**
news	**nuntius, -i** m
never	**numquam**
night	**nox, noctis** f
no one	**nemo, nullius**
not	**non; haud**
nothing	**nihil**

notice	**animadverto, -ere, -verti, -versum**
nourish	**alo, -ere, alui, altum (alitum)**
now	**nunc**; (= by now) **iam**
obey	**pareo** (2) + dative
old	**vetus, -eris**
old man	**senex, senis** m
once (upon a time)	**olim**
one	**unus, -a, -um**
only	**solum; modo**
not only…but also	**non solum (modo)…sed etiam**
order (*verb*)	**impero** (1); **iubeo, -ere, iussi, iussum**
order (*noun*)	**iussum, -i** n
by order of	**iussu** + gen.
others, the	**ceteri, -orum** m pl
ought	**debeo** (2)
our	**noster, -tra, -trum**
outside	**foris**
overcome	**supero** (1)
palace	**regia, -ae** f
Palatine	**Palatium, -ii** n
part, for my	**equidem**
penalty	**poena, -ae** f
pay the penalty	**poenas do, dare, dedi, datum**
people	**populus, -i** m
(common) people	**plebs, plebis** f
perhaps	**fortasse**
Persians	**Persae, -arum** m pl
pestilence	**pestilentia, -ae** f
Phalinus	**Phalinus, -i** m
pierce, transfix,	
run through	**transfigo, -ere, -fixi, -fictum**
pile up	**congero, -ere, -gessi, -gestum**
plan	**consilium, -ii** n
power	**imperium, -ii** n; **potestas, -atis** f
poppy	**papaver, -eris** n
Porta Capena	**Porta Capena, Portae Capenae** f
praetor	**praetor, -oris** m
praise	**laudo** (1)
pray	**precor** (1)
prayer	**votum, -i** n
prefer	**malo, malle, malui**
present, I am	**adsum, -esse, -fui**
prepare	**paro** (1)
pretend	**simulo** (1)
previous	**prior, -oris**
promise	**promitto, -ere, promisi, promissum; polliceor** (2)

prison	**carcer, -eris** m; or use **vincula, -orum** n pl
public	**publicus, -a -um**
quick	**celer, -eris, -ere**
raise	**tollo, -ere, sustuli, sublatum**
realise	**intellego, -ere, -exi, -ectum**
really	**re vera**
reason	**causa, -ae** f
receive	**accipio, -ere, -cepi, -ceptum**
recognise	**agnosco, -ere, agnovi, agnitum**; **cognosco**, etc
refresh	**reficio, -ere, -feci, -fectum**
reign	**regno** (1)
release	**libero** (1); **emitto, -ere, emisi, emissum**
relics, remains	**reliquiae, -arum** f pl
renew	**renovo** (1); **redintegro** (1)
reply (*verb*)	**respondeo, -ere, respondi, responsum**
reply (*noun*)	**responsum, -i** n
report back, relate	**refero, -ferre, rettuli, relatum**
rest, the	**ceteri, -ae, -a**
restore (= give back)	**reddo, -ere, reddidi, redditum**
retreat	**me recipio, -ere, -cepi, -ceptum; pedem refero, -ferre, rettuli, relatum**
return	**redeo, -ire, redii, reditum; regredior, -i, -gressus sum**
reveal	**patefacio, -ere, -feci, -factum**
Roman	**Romanus, -a, -um**
Rome	**Roma, -ae** f
Romulus	**Romulus, - i** m
root	**stirps, stirpis** f
ruin	**ruina, -ae** f
rush	**ruo, -ere, rui, rutum**
Sabines	**Sabini, -orum** m pl
sad	**tristis, -e**
safe	**tutus, -a, -um; incolumis, -e**
safety	**salus, -utis** f
save	**servo** (1)
say	**dico, -ere, dixi, dictum**
he said (*in dir. sp.*)	**inquit**
scarcely	**vix**
scout	**speculator, -oris** m
see	**video, -ere, vidi, visum**
seed	**semen, -inis** n
seem	**videor, -eri, visus sum**
senator	**senator, -oris** m; in pl = **patres, -um** m pl
send	**mitto, -ere, misi, missum**
send ahead	**praemitto, -ere, -misi, -missum**
self (*emphatic*)	**ipse, ipsa, ipsum**

Sequani	**Sequani, -orum** m pl
Seuthes	**Seuthes, -is** m
Sextus	**Sextus, -i** m
shield	**scutum, -i** n
ship	**navis, -is** f
shoulder	**umerus, -i** m
shout	**clamo** (1)
silence	**silentium, -ii** n
silent	**tacitus, -a, -um**
silent, I am	**taceo** (2); **sileo** (2)
since	**cum** + subj; **quoniam**
sister	**soror, -oris** f
sit	**sedeo, -ere, sedi, sessum**
sky	**caelum, -i** n
slaughter	**occido, -ere, occidi, occisum**; **trucido** (1)
slave	**servus, - i** m
slither, slip out	**elabor, -i, -lapsus sum**
small	**parvus, -a, -um**
snake	**serpens, -entis** m
so	**tam** (with adj. and adv.); **adeo** (with verbs)
so great	**tantus, -a, -um**
so many	**tot**
so often	**totiens**
soldier	**miles, -itis** m
some	**nonnulli, -ae, -a**
some ... others	**alii ... alii**
son	**filius, -ii** m
soon	**mox, brevi (tempore)**
as soon as	**simul atque (ac)**
speak	**loquor, -i, locutus sum**
speech	**oratio, -ionis** f
make a speech	**orationem habeo** (2)
spoils	**spolia, -orum** n pl
spot, on the	**ilico**
state	**respublica, reipublicae** f
stay	**maneo, -ere, -nsi, -nsum; moror** (1)
stay behind	**remaneo, -ere, -nsi, -nsum**
stealthily	**furtim**
stern	**severus, -a, -um**
stop, halt	**consisto, -ere, constiti**
strengthen	**confirmo** (1); **corroboro** (1)
strike	**percello, -ere, -culi, -culsum**
stupid	**stultus, -a -um**
such, of such a kind	**talis, -e**
suffer	**patior, -i, passus sum**
suppress	**comprimo, -ere, -pressi, -pressum**
supreme	**summus, -a, -um**
suspect	**suspicor** (1)

146

sword	**gladius, -ii** m
take	**capio, -ere, cepi, captum**
take possession of	**occupo** (1)
take to flight	**me fugae mando** (1)
Tarquinius	**Tarquinius, -ii** m
tear	**lacrima, -ae** f
tell	(= say) **dico, -ere, dixi, dictum**; (= order) **impero** (1) + dative; i**ubeo, -ere, iussi, iussum**; (= inform) **certiorem facio, -ere, feci, factum**
tent	**tabernaculum, -i** n
terrible	**atrox, -ocis**
terrify	**(per)terreo** (2)
than	**quam**
then	**tum**; (= next) **deinde**
there	**ibi**
from there	**inde**
therefore	**itaque**; **igitur** (2nd word)
thing	**res, rei** f
think	**puto** (1)
thinking	**ratus, -a, -um**
this	**hic, haec, hoc**
Thracian	**Thrax, Thracis**
three	**tres, tria**
threshold	**limen, inis** n
throng	**turba, -ae** f; **multitudo, -inis** f
through	**per** + acc.
throw	**conicio, -ere, -ieci, -iectum**
throw away	**abicio, -ere, -ieci, -iectum**
time	**tempus, -oris** n
time, for a long	**diu**
time, for a short	**paulisper**
Tissaphernes	**Tissaphernes, -is** m
Titus	**Titus, -i** m
tomorrow	**cras**
too	**quoque**
town	**oppidum, -i** n
travel	**iter facio, -ere, feci, factum; vehor, -i, vectus sum**
trial	**iudicium, -ii** n
tribunal	**tribunal, -alis** n
troops	**copiae, -arum** f pl
try	**conor** (1)
two	**duo, -ae, -o**
tyrannical	**regius, -a, -um**
unarmed	**inermis, -e**
uncle	**avunculus, -i** m
understand	**intellego, -ere, -xi, -ctum**

unhappy	**miser, -era, -erum**
unpopular	**invisus, -a, -um**
uproar	**tumultus, -us** m
valley	**valles, -is** f
valour	**virtus, -utis** f
victim (sacrificial)	**victima, -ae** f
victorious	**victor, -oris**
victory	**victoria, -ae** f
view, opinion	**sententia, -ae** f
villa	**villa, -ae** f
visit	**viso, -ere, visi, visum**; **visito** (1); **venio ad** + accusative
voice	**vox, vocis** f
Volscians	**Volsci, -orum** m pl
walk	**ambulo** (1)
want	**volo, velle, volui**
war	**bellum, -i** n
wage war	**bellum gero, -ere, gessi, gestum**
weakened	**fractus, -a, -um**
weapon	**telum, -i** n; *in pl* = **arma, -orum** n pl
well-disposed	**benevolus, -a, -um**
when	**ubi; cum**
whether...or	**sive (seu)...sive (seu)**
which ? (*of two*)	**uter, -tra, -trum**
why?	**cur**
wicked	**improbus, -a, -um**
willing, I am	**volo, velle, volui**
window	**fenestra, -ae** f
without	**sine** + ablative
wonder	**miror** (1)
wood	**silva, -ae** f
wooden	**ligneus, -a, -um**
word	**verbum, -i** n
young man	**iuvenis, -is** m
Zacynthian	**Zacynthius, -a, -um**

Also available

LATIN BEYOND GCSE

John Taylor

ISBN 978 1 85399 720 4

Latin Beyond GCSE covers all the linguistic requirements for the OCR AS-level in Latin, and the grammar for A2. The first part of the book introduces new constructions and the translation of sentences from English to Latin, with practice passages for unseen translation at AS standard. The next section introduces the translation and scansion of verse, and includes passages for unseen translation and comprehension at A2 standard in both prose and verse. This is followed by longer unadapted extracts from a range of prose authors. Finally there is a reference section including a summary of all constructions, a comprehensive grammar, and a vocabulary of 1000 Latin words (with an additional list of 250 common poetic words for A2 verse passages).

John Taylor is Head of Classics at Tonbridge School, Kent. He is the author of *Greek to GCSE Parts 1 and 2*, *Greek Beyond GCSE*, *Essential GCSE Latin* and (with Stephen Anderson) *Greek Unseen Translation*.

ESSENTIAL GCSE LATIN

John Taylor

ISBN 978 1 85399 693 1

Essential GCSE Latin is neither a complete course from scratch nor a reference grammar, but a summary of all the linguistic requirements for the OCR Examination Board specification (2007 onwards), aimed mainly at pupils in their GCSE year.

Whatever course they have used, many students remain very hazy about grammar. It is difficult to track back in a multi-volume course to the first introduction of a particular construction. Traditional grammars, on the other hand, can be forbidding, and often do not give enough help with syntax and idiom. This book breaks everything down into bite-sized chunks, with examples and practice sentences (650 in all) on each point, and generous cross-referencing. It concentrates on the understanding of principles in both accidence and syntax, in order to cut down on rote learning. Practice passages for the optional harder unseen translation passage are included.

John Taylor is Head of Classics at Tonbridge School, Kent. He is the author of *Greek to GCSE Parts 1 and 2*, *Greek Beyond GCSE*, *Latin Beyond GCSE* and (with Stephen Anderson) *Greek Unseen Translation*.

WRITING LATIN

Richard Ashdowne and James Morwood

ISBN 978 1 85399 701 3

A new guide to writing in Latin, this accessible book displays the following features:

- **Broad coverage** – all the major grammatical constructions of the Latin language are covered, reinforcing what students have learnt from reading Latin.
- **Thorough accessible explanations** – no previous experience of writing in Latin is assumed.
- **Hundreds of user-friendly examples** – clear accurate illustrations of the constructions described, all with full translations.
- **Over six hundred practice sentences** – graduated exercises leading students through three levels of difficulty from elementary to advanced level.
- **Introduction to Latin word order** – a brief guide to some of the most important principles.
- **Longer passages for practising continuous prose composition** – more challenging passages to stretch the most able students.
- **Commentaries on examples of Latin prose style** – passages from great Latin prose writers focus attention on imitating real Latin usage.
- **Complete list of vocabulary** – all the words needed for the exercises and a valuable reference for English-Latin work in general.

Richard Ashdowne read Classics at New College, Oxford and is now engaged in research in linguistics at Oxford.

James Morwood is an Emeritus Fellow of Wadham College, Oxford. He is the author of several books, including *The Plays of Euripides* published by Duckworth.

GREEK TO GCSE

John Taylor

Part 1 ISBN 1 85399 656 6
Part 2 ISBN 1 85399 703 7

This two-volume course was written in response to a JACT survey of over a hundred schools. The course offers a fast-track route to GCSE for those with limited time. Based on experience of what pupils find difficult, it concentrates on the essentials, and on the understanding of principles in both accidence and syntax. It aims to be user-friendly, but also to give pupils a firm foundation for further study.

Part 1 covers the basics: the main declensions, a range of active tenses, and a vocabulary of 275 Greek words to be learned. Confidence is built up by constant consolidation of the material. Each chapter concentrates on stories with one source or subject: Aesop, the *Odyssey*, and Alexander the Great. The first volume is self-contained, with its own reference section.

Part 2 introduces a wider range of grammatical forms and constructions. Its revised edition completes the coverage of requirements for the current GCSE, expanding vocabulary to 480 words. Reading material moves from Socrates and the Sophists to the world of myth, and finally to extended passages of lightly adapted Herodotus. Practice passages and revision sentences for GCSE complete Part 2, which has a reference section covering the whole course.

John Taylor is Head of Classics at Tonbridge School, Kent. He is the author of *Greek Beyond GCSE, Essential GCSE Latin, Latin Beyond GCSE* and (with Stephen Anderson) *Greek Unseen Translation*.

GREEK BEYOND GCSE

John Taylor

ISBN 978 1 85399 704 4

This book covers all the linguistic requirements for AS-level, and aims to bring students to a point where they can tackle original Greek texts with confidence. It is designed as continuation of *Greek to GCSE*, but is self-contained and can be used independently. The first part of the book introduces new constructions accompanied by exercises and lightly adapted reading passages. This is followed by extended extracts from a range of prose authors, unadapted except by minor omission. Finally there is a reference section including a summary of all constructions, a comprehensive grammar, and a vocabulary of 830 Greek words.

John Taylor is Head of Classics at Tonbridge School, Kent. He is the author of *Greek to GCSE Parts 1 and 2*, *Essential GCSE Latin*, *Latin Beyond GCSE* and (with Stephen Anderson) *Greek Unseen Translation*.

GREEK UNSEEN TRANSLATION

Stephen Anderson and John Taylor

ISBN 978 1 85399 684 9

Greek Unseen Translation consists of 120 passages from Ancient Greek authors.

The first half of the book contains twenty adapted passages building up to GCSE level, thirty lightly adapted ones for AS, and ten easy unadapted passages to introduce the translation of verse.

The second half contains thirty prose and thirty verse passages of A2 standard, unadapted except by minor omissions. Vocabulary beyond the core assumed at each level is glossed.

Stephen Anderson is Senior Tutor and former Head of Classics at Winchester College.

John Taylor is Head of Classics at Tonbridge School, Kent. He is the author of *Greek to GCSE Parts 1 and 2*, *Greek Beyond GCSE*, *Essential GCSE Latin* and *Latin Beyond GCSE*.